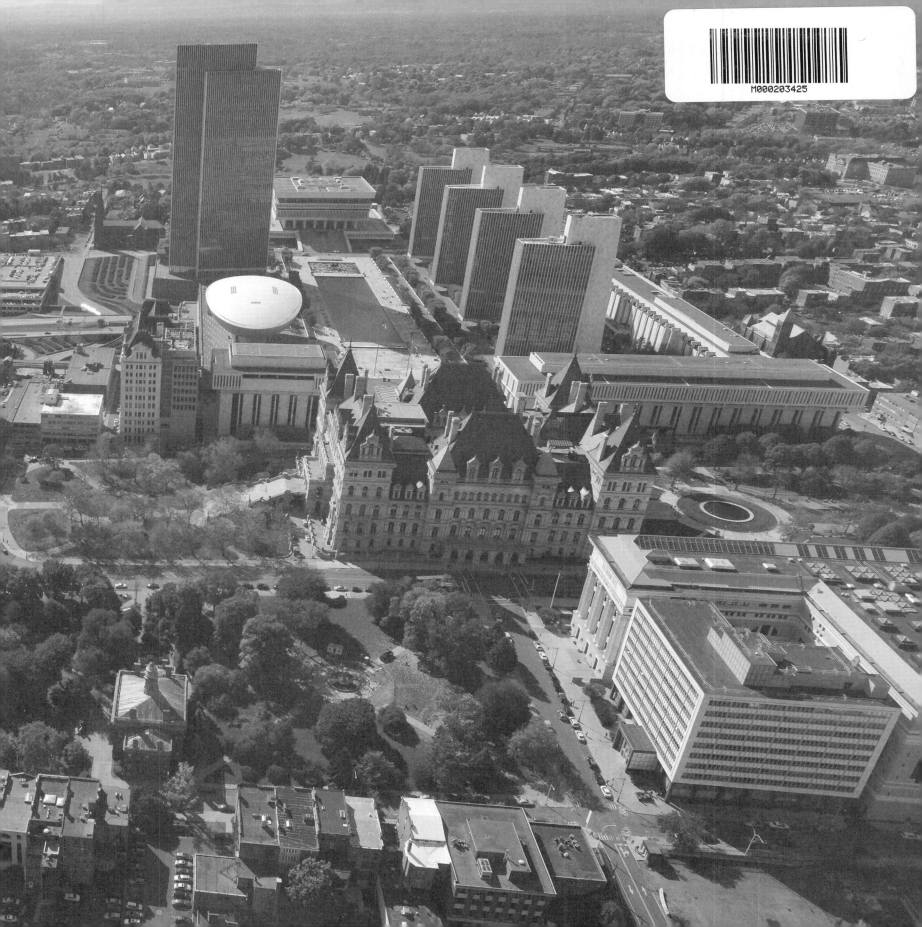
M000203425

CAPITOL STORY

THIRD EDITION

CAPITOL STORY

THIRD EDITION

C. R. Roseberry

with revisions and additional research by the
NEW YORK STATE OFFICE OF GENERAL SERVICES
and a new chapter by
DIANA S. WAITE
new photography by
GARY DAVID GOLD

FOREWORD BY
GOVERNOR ANDREW M. CUOMO

EXCELSIOR EDITIONS
AN IMPRINT OF STATE UNIVERSITY OF NEW YORK PRESS

Published by
STATE UNIVERSITY OF NEW YORK PRESS, ALBANY

© 1964, 1982, 2014 State of New York

All rights reserved
Printed in the United States of America

No part of this book may be used or reproduced in any manner
whatsoever without written permission. No part of this book may be stored
in a retrieval system or transmitted in any form or by any means including electronic,
electrostatic, magnetic tape, mechanical, photocopying, recording, or otherwise
without the prior permission in writing of the publisher.

EXCELSIOR EDITIONS
IS AN IMPRINT OF STATE UNIVERSITY OF NEW YORK PRESS

For information, contact State University of New York Press, Albany, NY
www.sunypress.edu

Production and book design, Laurie Searl
Marketing, Fran Keneston

Library of Congress Cataloging-in-Publication Data

Roseberry, Cecil R.
Capitol story / C.R. Roseberry and Diana S. Waite. — Third edition.
pages cm. — (Excelsior editions)
Includes bibliographical references and index.
ISBN 978-1-4384-5639-3 (hardcover : alk. paper)
ISBN 978-1-4384-5641-6 (ebook)
1. New York State Capitol (Albany, N.Y.)
2. Public buildings—New York (State)—Albany. I. Waite, Diana S. II. Title.
F129.A38N487 2015
974.7'43—dc23
2014024828

10 9 8 7 6 5 4 3 2 1

Publication of this edition of *Capitol Story* was made
possible with the support of Furthermore, a program
of the J. M. Kaplan Fund; the Gerry Charitable Trust;
Richard J. Miller Jr.; Simpson Gumpertz & Heger; the
Bender Family Foundation, and Matthew Bender IV.

CONTENTS

STATE OF NEW YORK

EXECUTIVE CHAMBER

ALBANY 12224

ANDREW M. CUOMO
GOVERNOR

Dear Reader:

New York State's Capitol is a monument in every sense of the word. Its beauty honors the spirit of innovation of the New Yorkers who built it, its function honors the democratic principles upon which our state was founded, and most importantly, its purpose honors the call to public service that characterizes the women and men who work inside of it. That is why understanding the Capitol's story gives us greater insight into New York's story.

When I became Governor, my first act was to issue Executive Order #1, which removed the barricades surrounding the Capitol and reopened the Executive Chamber to the public. I believed then, as I do now, that this is the people's building and they merely place it in trust to me and the legislative leaders. Ensuring that every New Yorker can come here and watch their government in action is one of my most important duties as Governor.

Unfortunately in 2011, the Capitol was not in a condition worthy of its heritage and the pride of the New Yorkers who visited. For over a decade, restoration projects were languishing and necessary renovations were being left undone. Shortly after I assumed office, I made it a priority to expedite these projects, thereby saving taxpayers millions of dollars while simultaneously returning the Capitol to a place worthy of being the center of government for the Empire State.

State government is working, and today, New Yorkers can be proud of everything that has been accomplished. Nearly four years after I issued my first Executive Order, we eliminated a $10 billion deficit and turned it into a $2 billion surplus, expanded civil rights, passed four on-time budgets and made our state stronger economically than it has been in decades.

The Capitol is once again as powerful a symbol for New York State government as it was when it was first constructed. It is a tangible example of the good that government can do. I hope that as you read about New York's Capitol you will appreciate our government, people, culture, and history.

Sincerely,

ANDREW M. CUOMO

WE WORK FOR THE PEOPLE
PERFORMANCE ★ INTEGRITY ★ PRIDE

♻ printed on recycled paper

STATE OF NEW YORK
EXECUTIVE CHAMBER
ALBANY

NELSON A. ROCKEFELLER
GOVERNOR

FOREWORD

The State Capitol at Albany is an extraordinary building, a repository of some important chapters of our history, and rich in irreplaceable architecture of a bygone era.

Hemmed in for decades by row houses, it is reemerging today as one of the focal points of a great new redevelopment project, on which the State of New York and the City of Albany are cooperating, to create a fitting capital for the Empire State. It is therefore doubly appropriate that its colorful history should be published at this time.

In compiling this volume, the editors and staff were extremely fortunate in having the unstinting assistance and counsel of Dr. Albert B. Corey, who served New York State as its Historian for nineteen years. As the book neared completion, Dr. Corey prepared the cogent introduction which follows this foreword. It proved to be one of his last services to the State he had served with such ability and devotion. Tragically, on November 10, 1963, he succumbed to injuries from an automobile accident. "Capitol Story" is therefore, in a very real sense, a memorial, and a fitting one, to this distinguished public servant, whose work over the years enhanced the lives of all the residents of the State.

"Capitol Story" is an absorbing narrative. It adds a colorful and significant chapter to our State's history, and is certain to elicit new appreciation and understanding of a unique building, the Capitol of the Empire State.

Nelson A. Rockefeller
Governor

INTRODUCTION

TO THE FIRST EDITION

No one is ever lukewarm in his opinion of the Capitol in Albany. Either he looks upon it as an atrocity of jumbled architecture or he enjoys it as a successful blending of architectural forms which is esthetically pleasing. Perhaps those who dislike the Capitol are architectural purists who demand that a building follow a single style from foundation to roof or they believe state capitols should have domes. Since objectors are much more vocal in their dislke than those who approve, the approval, which is quite as sharply but less vociferously expressed, is sometimes drowned out.

This book has been written not to redress the balance between the two but to tell the story of a building which is unique among state capitols in the United States. It took thirty years to build, it is the product of three groups of architects, and it cost far more than any other capitol. It is so solidly built that the Civil Defense authorities are hard put to find any shelter that exceeds its protective qualities.

The Capitol was begun in an era when European forms still dominated the design of public buildings in the United States. It was completed a score of years after the age of structural steel had begun. The thirty years between the end of the Civil War and the turn of the century witnessed a wave of expansionism, experimentation, and innovation throughout the country, and nowhere more so than in New York. This ferment affected industry, busioness, government, education, and the arts. Old forms were not discarded completely, rather they were changed and modified to express the cultural needs of the time. It is into this framework, as an expression of an age, that the architectural variations

Postcard of the Capitol, ca. 1900

of the Capitol must be placed to be understood and appreciated. The Capitol is a symbol of an era when change was in the air.

The compelling quality of this book is that the author, drawing on a wealth of contemporary sources of fact and opinion, has written a critical, objective, and yet sympathetic story of the Capitol. It leads to an understanding of Lieutenant Governor William Dorsheimer's statement in 1876 that the building should be "A school of architecture in itself to the people of the State."

Albert B. Corey
State Historian from 1944 to 1963

East Capitol Park

CHAPTER ONE

CHATEAU ON A HILL

Governor Frank Black

WINTER WITHHELD ITS COLD BREATH THAT YEAR AS IF PURPOSELY TO HELP ALONG the hurried work of finishing the new Capitol. Crews labored in day and night shifts. They would have been working Sundays, too, except that some religious organizations protested.

The sheds of stonecutters and masons came down. Rubble was whisked away. The premises were raw and muddy—no walks, no landscaping. But in late December 1897 New Yorkers could finally get a clear look at the fabulous structure on the hill to which so much of their tax money had gone. There had never been such a building!

The reason for the sudden haste was the determination of Governor Frank S. Black to walk up the seventy seven steps of the Eastern Approach of the Capitol on the first day of the New Year and open the front door. It would be a symbolic public act and at the same time give him a great deal of personal satisfaction.

For almost twenty years the state government had been operating without a front door—ever since the old Capitol was vacated. The new Capitol had been in gradually increasing use during that time, though incomplete. Access was gained via side entrances not yet dignified by porticos.

Governor Black had vowed to finish the Capitol during his term. In his January 1, 1897, inaugural message to the State Legislature he had said:

This subject may well be approached with reluctance. It is about thirty years since the building was started, and over $22,000,000 have been appropriated and spent or sunk. It has dragged itself through nearly a third of a century, always clamoring for money, until the people have nearly despaired of its completion and have come to regard it as an affliction from which time affords but little hope of relief. If an individual or a corporation had managed an undertaking as this has been man-aged, they would have been discredited years ago. . . . This building ought to be finished at once. The work should be done by contract, and sufficient money appropriated to pay for it. The State needs the structure for its uses, but it needs still more to escape the scandal of a building of enormous cost and unparalleled extravagance undergoing at the same time the process of construction at one end and decay at the other.[1]

At the end of Black's first year in office, the Capitol was not yet finished, but the end was in sight. The superb front flight of steps—the Eastern Approach—was done, except for some carving.

Eastern Approach, looking southeast toward State Street, ca. 1890s

The construction of the Capitol had dominated Albany life since the Civil War. An entire generation had grown up since it was begun. It had taken as long to erect as the Great Pyramid of Cheops. It had cost twice as much as the U.S. Capitol at Washington.[2] Controversy had swirled around it. Long before it had reached this stage, its fame had spread throughout the world. Travelers came to gaze at it, unfinished as it was. Magazine pieces were written about it. Governor Lucius Robinson had called it a public calamity. Friendlier observers saw it as the country's most interesting public building. It was the expression of an era of American life. It was a veritable school of architecture and museum of stone carving. Perhaps nowhere else was there a building in which architecture and politics had been so closely intertwined. In one instance, the style of its architecture actually had been legislated.

It had another uniqueness: it did not look as a Capitol was supposed to look. Almost by unwritten law, Capitol buildings in the United States had domes. This one was conspicuously domeless.

Situated at the top of the rise from the Hudson River, it had somewhat the aspect of a New World castle, a quality accentuated by its whiteness. The light hued Maine granite so carefully selected for its exterior was as yet unsullied by atmospheric grime. The plateau on which it stood was 150 feet above the river's tidewater, and the face of the building rose more than 100 feet still higher. The imposing effect was magnified by the fact that it was taller than any other building in the city.

Instead of a dome, the skyline of this unconventional Capitol had four corner pavilions accented with red tiled pyramidal roofs punctuated by handsome dormers and tall chimney stacks. The building's style of architecture might take some untangling. But the roof features provided valid and striking architectural comparison—to a French Renaissance chateau of the reign of Francis I.

The building had been a steadily growing problem for ten governors before Governor Black inherited it in 1897. Ground

**George W. Aldridge,
Superintendent of Public Works**

was broken under Reuben Fenton in 1867, and John T. Hoffman laid the cornerstone in 1871. John A. Dix and Samuel J. Tilden watched its walls rise. Lucius Robinson so detested the building that he refused to move in when the north central section of the building was opened, and thus it remained for Alonzo B. Cornell to be the first to use the executive suite. Reform minded Grover Cleveland tried to speed things up by putting an experienced builder architect in charge. David B. Hill fought to keep that official's hands from being tied and then sweated through the scandal of the Assembly Chamber ceiling. Roswell P. Flower signed appropriations with the refrain that "the wisest economy now is to complete the building."[3] Levi P. Morton instigated a private contract system instead of day labor but had trouble getting it rolling.

Frank Black, a prosperous lawyer from Troy, was a tall, spare man of scholarly mien. A gift for oratory had helped him in politics; when the Republicans ran him for governor in 1896, one of his campaign promises was to finish up "that building" on the Albany hill. Soon after his election, the New York Tribune editorialized: "There are two things which the State Capitol at Albany may confidently be relied on to furnish: an enduring opportunity to spend large sums of money, and an occasion for speculation as to when, if ever, the huge pile will be finished."[4]

Governor Black quickly got a compliant Legislature to abolish the existing Capitol Commission and to transfer its powers to the state superintendent of public works, who was then to complete the Capitol "by contract."[5] He was George W. Aldridge, an experienced building contractor from Rochester, as well as the aggressive political boss of Monroe County. The contracts that Aldridge awarded stipulated that the Eastern Approach and the main entrance must be finished before January 1, 1898. Hence the hectic work with the day and night crews. The abnormally mild weather was a godsend. There was no serious snow until the last day of 1897.

On New Year's morning Governor Black rode up to the Eagle Street edge of the undeveloped space that would become

The east facade of the Capitol during the final phases
of construction, looking up State Street, 1895

Capitol after completion, looking up State Street, 1900

East Capitol Park. There a select group of dignitaries awaited. Superintendent Aldridge had laid a plank walk across the frozen mud to the foot of the staircase.

The governor led a small procession across the planks, up the middle of the staircase, and under the groin vaults. Beside him walked, on the one hand, Superintendent Aldridge, on the other, the governor's son, Arthur. The attorney general and his staff followed and then the heads of various other State departments. The march was flanked by a squad of police guards.

At the New Year's reception in the Executive Chamber, Governor Black accepted plaudits, and the talk was mainly about how fast the work on the Capitol had been done in the past nine months. This year in his annual message to the legislature, Governor Black declared that "There will be no further alteration. The structure will be completed, the sheds torn down and the walks laid out, before the first day of next October. There has not been a time in the last fifteen years that reasonable effort would not have accomplished these things in twenty-four months."[6]

The Spanish American War flared that summer. A special session of the Legislature was called to decide how New York should play its part. In spite of this interruption, the governor kept his promise about the Capitol.

In July there was a decisive charge up San Juan Hill in Cuba. The hero of it returned home to be elected governor of New York. Theodore Roosevelt was the first governor to take the oath of office in the finished Capitol.

Old Capitol, designed by Philip Hooker and built in 1806–1809

CHAPTER TWO

THEMIS DETHRONED

January term of the 1781 Legislature
was held in the old Stadt Huys.

THE OLD CAPITOL WAS A HATBOX COMPARED WITH THE NEW. MEEKLY IT STOOD while the granite facades of its successor grew behind it until they shut off the afternoon sun. The shadow was prophetic of doom. A journalist wrote that the condemned relic "seemed to crouch at the feet of the new edifice," that it looked "diminutive, humble—almost mean."[1]

New York's earlier Capitol had the aura of a frayed but beloved antique, with a four-pillared Grecian portico and a cupola rather than a dome. Affixed to the flagpole above the portico was a "time ball," electrically controlled, which dropped daily at the stroke of noon. And perched atop its cupola was a wooden statue of Themis, 11 feet tall. Themis was the Greek goddess of divine justice, outfitted with a pair of balances and a sword.

The figure of Themis was sculpted by John Dixey as a replica of one he had done in 1815 to grace the cupola of New York's new city hall. The copy for Albany was hoisted to the apex of the Capitol a year later. An Irish artist, born at Dublin and trained in London, Dixey landed at Philadelphia in 1789 and migrated to New York in 1801. In America he turned to wood carving for a livelihood, copying busts and setting up a studio for architectural decoration. The images of Justice in New York and Albany were his best-known works when he died in 1820.

One night, shortly before the old Capitol was scheduled for the wrecker's ball, a thunderstorm toppled Themis. She crashed to the sidewalk.

Nostalgic tears were shed over the building in which governors DeWitt Clinton, Martin Van Buren, and William H. Seward had presided; which had played so major a part in the rise of the Whig Party; where Lafayette had been lionized and Abraham Lincoln had spoken. Reviewing its past, a newspaper mourned: "It was a liberal education in the political history of New York to know the old Capitol."[2]

Albany had become the capital city almost by accident. New York had been the seat of colonial government until it was captured by the British. The seat of government shifted from Harlem to White Plains to Fishkill, then veered between Poughkeepsie, Kingston, and Albany. After the Revolution the Legislature continued to "meet around." New York, and Albany competed for the honor of becoming the permanent capital. In Albany the sessions were held in the ancient Dutch Stadt Huys, which served as city hall and courthouse.

Government breeds records and documents. It became decidedly inconvenient to transport the necessary papers back and forth. When it met at the Stadt Huys in 1797, the Legislature passed a bill for erecting "a public building" at Albany for the storage of

Senate Chamber in the old Capitol

"records, books, papers, and other things."[3] This building, known as the State Hall, was by no means a capitol—but it meant that the Legislature was putting down roots in Albany.

The proposal to erect a "state-house" in Albany came to a head in 1804, when the city offered to donate a lot on its public square and also to shoulder part of the cost in return for sharing its use. The public square was a well-trodden, open rectangle at the top of State Street hill, long used as a recreational and parade ground. It commanded a pleasant view of the sail-studded Hudson and the rolling hills beyond. The Legislature accepted.

A favored way of raising public moneys when taxable resources were sparse was the lottery. The cost of the building was $110,685.42. Of this amount, $32,000 was raised from lotteries.

There chanced to be in Albany a designer of buildings, Philip Hooker, who already had a wide reputation. He was selected for the job. Hooker had learned his profession from his father and was a practical architect. His style was to be greatly admired in future years as typical of "American classicism." Only two of his buildings survive in Albany—the North Dutch Reformed Church on North Pearl Street and the Joseph Henry

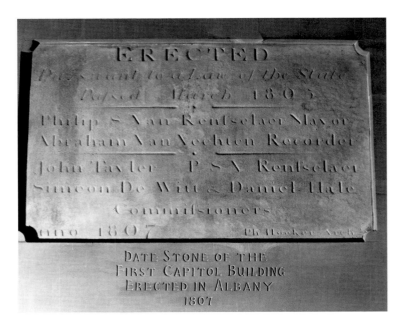

Cornerstone of the old Capitol,
now part of the Great Western Staircase at the fourth level

Memorial (originally the Albany Academy), which stands just north of the present Capitol.

The cornerstone of the Capitol was laid in 1806 by Mayor Philip Schuyler Van Rensselaer, a son of the patroon, Stephen Van Rensselaer. While the building was going up, Robert Fulton moored his steamboat at the waterfront below.

The Capitol built by Hooker faced squarely down Albany's broad central thoroughfare to the river. It was more impressive by virtue of its location than by size. The Ionic portico gave it a flavor more Grecian than "American classic." But the cupola was distinctively Hooker.

The building was occupied in 1809. Not just the State moved in—but the mayor of Albany, the City Council, and the county Board of Supervisors. This arrangement could not last indefinitely. In 1829 the State bought out the city's interest for $17,500. Albany applied the money to erecting a city hall, also designed by Philip Hooker.

Strangely enough, no law was passed designating Albany as the capital city. An 1809 act appropriated $5,000 "for the completion of the public building, which building shall hereafter be denominated 'The Capitol.'"[4] The oversight was not corrected until 1971 when the Legislature placed a statute on the books declaring: "The capital city of the State of New York is hereby designated to be the city of Albany."[5] The bill's sponsor was Assemblyman Charles Henderson of Hornell, Steuben County, who discovered the omission.

Agitation began as early as 1829 to relocate the capital city—preferably to the more geographic center of the state. Utica and Syracuse were most frequently mentioned as possibilities. The Erie Canal had been dug, the railroads soon were spinning their web, and people flowed into the hitherto sparsely populated hinterlands. Cities such as Buffalo and Rochester sprang up. Legislators from the western counties found themselves at a disadvantage in traveling to and from Albany.

Meanwhile, dissatisfaction with the Capitol building grew apace. Even with the City having moved out, expanding State activities stretched its seams. The chambers were ill-ventilated. Committees were named to study their shortcomings. One reported that the legislators habitually complained of dizziness caused by poor quality air.

Governor's Chamber in the old Capitol

Assembly Chamber

A separate building to house the State Library was erected in 1854, fronting on State Street behind the Capitol. Until then, the library, whose main function was to serve the Legislature and State agencies, had been cramped in three rooms on the second and third floors of the Capitol. Its new quarters, a narrow, two-story structure, was connected to the main floor of the Capitol by an umbilical corridor and could hardly be termed commodious.

When the Civil War was at its height, in 1863, state senator James A. Bell, from Dexter in Jefferson County, began agitating for a new Capitol, with this resolution: "That it be referred to the Trustees of the Capitol and the chairman of the committee on public buildings, to procure suitable plans for a new capitol, with adequate accommodations for the several purposes for which the same is needed, and to report to the next Legislature."[6]

The chairman of the Senate's committee on public buildings was John V. L. Pruyn, an eminent Albanian and zealous advocate of a new Capitol. Senator Bell was a member of that committee, and Pruyn wrote in his private journal that he had suggested the resolution to Bell. A scion of early Dutch aristocracy, Pruyn was the able attorney who drafted the consolidation plan for the New York Central Railroad, became its counsel, and was a power in the Democratic hierarchy known as the Albany Regency. He was also chancellor of the State Board of Regents, the governing body of the state's educational system.

Pruyn led an active social life and frequently entertained fellow legislators and high state officials at his luxurious home on nearby Elk Street, mingling politics with hospitality. As the result of one such meeting in April 1863, Pruyn was authorized by the Ways and Means Committee and the Senate Finance Committee to begin purchasing the properties on State Street to the rear of the Capitol, as far as Hawk Street. The acquisitions were made discreetly and quickly, before plans for a new state-house were publicized, to avoid inflated prices. Pruyn carried through the scheme mainly at his own expense, to the amount of $65,000, on the understanding that he would be reimbursed from the supply bill when titles were turned over to the State. Concerning the arrangement, Pruyn wrote in his journal that "This is the most important measure ever taken towards fixing the seat of government here permanently."[7]

In August 1863, an advertisement inviting architects to submit designs for a new Capitol was placed in newspapers, over Pruyn's signature. Only three firms responded, one being Fuller and Jones, architects of the Parliament building being erected at Ottawa, Canada; the other two were Gage Inslee and Rembrandt Lockwood, both of New York City. The three designs were examined by members of the Committee on Public

Second floor of the first State Library building

Buildings in February 1864, and Pruyn commented that the Fuller and Jones plan "was considered altogether the most satisfactory." No money accompanied the Senate resolution, and nothing came of these first designs.

Pruyn also inquired into the probable cost of acquiring Congress Hall Square to add to the State Street lots. Congress Hall was a popular hotel, which, by long usage, had become virtually an annex to the Capitol, and its removal would extend the State acquisitions through to Washington Avenue. The rambling hostelry, a favored haunt of legislators, faced onto Park Place, a north-south street cutting through the block behind the Capitol and the State Library.

The case against the old Capitol was summed up by a legislator from the floor:

Sir, when this building was originally completed, it was doubtless the most prominent and attractive feature of Albany. Dwarfed by its surroundings and depreciated by contrast, it has long since become an offense to the eye and a reproach to the State.

At an expenditure of more than one million pounds sterling, the Canadians have treated themselves with a Parliament House at Ottawa, the boast and fame of which fill the Continent. . . . It is said the State of New York is poor, and cannot afford to have a decent Capitol. Sir, I deny it. The State of New York is rich, and can afford to have a decent Capitol. One that shall fairly meet her wants, and correspond with her rank and power.[8]

On January 26, 1865, a bill was introduced in the Senate entitled "An Act authorizing the erection of a new Capitol." Its sponsor was an Albany attorney, Senator Ira Shafer. Less than two weeks later, a young freshman senator from Syracuse, Andrew D. White, set forth a bill "to establish the Cornell University, and to appropriate to it the income of the sale of public lands granted to the State by Congress."[9] It is relevant to observe that the new Capitol and the new university were hatched together, and cloakroom politics affected the fate of both bills. White was allied with Ezra Cornell, a new senator from Ithaca, who had made millions with the Western Union Telegraph Company.

The old question as to whether the Capitol should be in Albany remained, and the State determined to settle it once and for all. On January 27 a select committee of the Senate was appointed "to ascertain by correspondence, or otherwise, with the city of Buffalo and other municipalities of the State, on what terms the grounds and buildings necessary for a new Capitol and public offices can be obtained."[10] An inquiry was sent to all cities and more than two hundred villages. Some replied with tongue-in-cheek humor, some with outright sarcasm. Few took it seriously.

The village of Argyle invited the Capitol on the score that "It is a very moral and religious place, and can be recommended as a location on account of presenting no temptations to legislators to depart from the paths of virtue." The village president of Whitesboro wrote that "If the location of the capital of the

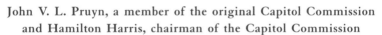

John V. L. Pruyn, a member of the original Capitol Commission and Hamilton Harris, chairman of the Capitol Commission

Empire State is to be put up to the highest bidder, like the yearly State Fair or the poor-house of a county, then, and in that case, the village of Whitesboro is not a competitor." Buffalo was not interested. The mayor of Utica skeptically responded that "any proposition we could make would not influence the moving of a brick from the present location."[11] Yonkers and Saratoga offered specific sites.

New York City, Albany's old rival, was very much in the market. Its aldermen voted to make a site available in Central Park or at the Battery, Tompkins Square, or Mount Morris Square—and were ready to throw in a spot for an Executive Mansion on Fifth Avenue.

The Legislature had made its gesture. Albany had no intention of letting the Capitol get away. Its Common Council took a vote and notified the State it was willing to "purchase and convey to the State of New York . . . the block of ground known as the Congress Hall block, or any other lands in the city required for such purposes."[12]

The Senate committee that sent the feelers throughout the State concluded that "to remove the Capitol from Albany at this time would not be justifiable, and from the character of the majority of the letters received, and the refusal of many cities and villages to reply to the circular of the committee, we think it cannot be desired by the people generally."[13]

While this exercise was going on, the bill creating Cornell University ran into trouble. A bevy of small colleges around the state, chiefly sectarian, sent agents to Albany, putting in their own claims for slices of the Morrill Land Grant. The Morrill Act of Congress, lately signed by President Abraham Lincoln, granted vast tracts of public lands in the West to Eastern states to

Congress Hall, a hotel that was demolished to build the new Capitol, *left*

Old Capitol during demolition, 1883

support education in agriculture and the "mechanic arts." New York's share was almost a million acres, and the Cornell project depended upon all of it. Lobbying pressures swayed many legislators, and the Cornell bill was bottled up in committees. Young Senator White proved a fast learner in politics, and Ezra Cornell was a tough fighter. At the showdown, after their bill finally passed in the Assembly, it was blocked in a Senate committee. With strong supporters, White was able to hold up the Capitol bill in committee, refusing to report it out until the Cornell bill was released for vote. His tactic worked. The act creating Cornell University triumphed on March 21, 1865.

The Senate passed the Capitol bill on March 31 and sent it to the Assembly. The lower house debated and returned the bill on April 28, with certain amendments, including a provision that the governor appoint three "New Capitol Commissioners" to solicit architectural designs and start the project moving and another that within three years the city of Albany deposit with the Land Office a deed to the "Congress Hall Block."

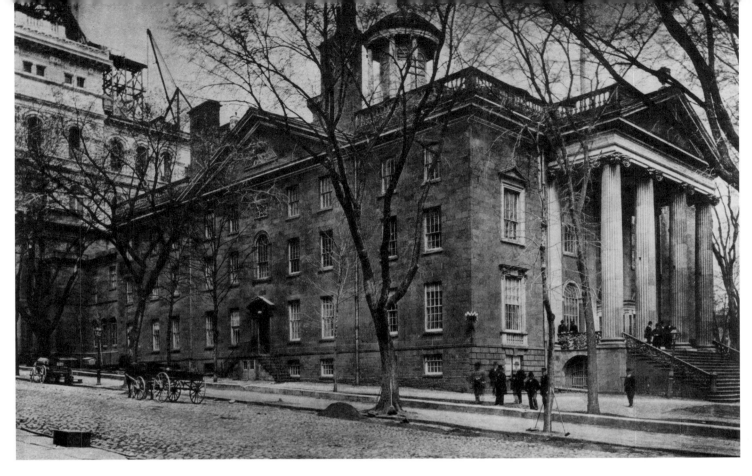

Old Capitol, with the new Capitol being constructed behind it

The proprietor of Congress Hall, under lease from the owners, was Adam Blake, a highly esteemed and well-to-do black man. His considerable fortune had been made as a restaurateur and caterer, as well as in real estate dealings. Blake had been given a good start in that career by his father, Adam Sr., who had been a house slave of the Van Rensselaer Manor and body servant to the last patroon, Stephen Van Rensselaer, who had set him free. Upon taking charge of the famed hotel earlier in 1865, Blake had enlarged it by connecting three adjacent brick residences on Park Place and furbishing them in sumptuous style. While neither the old Capitol nor Congress Hall stood on the actual ground needed for the new Capitol, their locations would be required eventually for construction staging and for Capitol Park.

The city lost no time in fulfilling its pledge. On June 1, 1865, the city purchased the lot on which Congress Hall stood, between Washington Avenue and Spring Street, for $125,000, and conveyed the title to the State of New York on October 4, 1865. An additional strip between Congress Hall and Hawk Street was acquired by the State in January 1866 for $61,000. Hawk Street was later agreed upon as the center line of the new Capitol.

Adam Blake's lease of Congress Hall was continued under both the city and the State until its demolition in 1878. Meanwhile, Blake arranged to have a fine new hotel erected on North Pearl Street—the Kenmore.

Governor Reuben E. Fenton appointed as the three original commissioners John V. L. Pruyn, a Democrat and by then a member of Congress; Hamilton Harris, a Republican and a prominent Albany attorney; and Obadiah B. Latham of Seneca Falls, a state senator and veteran contractor. The commissioners then chose Hamilton Harris as chairman.

Canadian Parliament Building, Center Block, 1859 design by Thomas Fuller and Chilion Jones

CHAPTER THREE

THE DESIGN COMPETITIONS

STATE OF NEW YORK.

PLANS FOR A NEW CAPITOL.

In pursuance of a Resolution of the Senate of this State, adopted on the twenty-fourth day of April last, by which it was referred to the Trustees of the Capitol (being the Governor, the Lieutenant Governor, the Speaker of the Assembly, the Secretary of State, the Attorney General, and the Comptroller,) and the Chairman of the Committee of the Senate on Public Buildings, to procure suitable plans for a new Capitol, with adequate accommodations for the several purposes for which the same is needed, and to report to the next Legislature, the Board named invite the presentation of plans for the erection of a NEW CAPITOL.

The Building should contain suitable Rooms for the following named Public Officers and purposes:—

1. The Governor and his Civil and Military Staff.
2. The Senate and its Officers and Committees.
3. The Assembly and its Officers and Committees.
4. The Court of Appeals, the Judges, Clerk and Officers of the Court.
5. The State Library.
6. The Superintendent of Public Instruction.
7. The Keeper of the Capitol, Store Rooms and Rooms for miscellaneous purposes needed in a building of this character.

More particular information as to the accommodations and arrangements which are considered desirable is contained in a printed Statement which will be forwarded by Post on application to the undersigned.

Special attention is requested to the best arrangements for heating, lighting and ventilation.

No appropriation was made for compensation for plans which may be prepared under the resolution of the Senate, and be considered meritorious, but the Trustees of the Capitol will recommend to the Legislature such provision for this purpose, as may be deemed proper.

Plans may be addressed to the undersigned at any time before the twentieth day of December next.

By order, JOHN V. L. PRUYN,
Chairman Senate Committee on Public Buildings.
Albany, August 31, 1863.

Newspaper advertisement announcing the design competition for the new Capitol, 1863

THOMAS FULLER, WHO WOULD BECOME THE FIRST DESIGNER OF THE CAPITOL, was a Briton who studied architecture in Bath and London and moved to the West Indies island of Antigua in 1845 to build a cathedral. He returned to England, but when he was thirty-four years old, he fared forth to try his fortune in Canada. Luck sailed with him.

Landing in Toronto in 1857, he formed a partnership with architect Chilion Jones. Canada was in the ferment of becoming a dominion. Cities were vying to be its capital. Queen Victoria arbitrated the choice. With some diplomatic prompting, she selected Ottawa, a lumber settlement on a bluff by the Ottawa River.[1] In 1859 a design competition was announced for a cluster of Parliament buildings. Fuller & Jones entered and won the commission for the center block. The design of that stately Gothic Revival ensemble in the wilderness caught the popular imagination and vaulted Fuller into sudden renown.

When it was advertised that New York State was contemplating a new Capitol, Thomas Fuller, residing in Ottawa, began submitting designs.

While the 1863 Fuller & Jones design was considered "most satisfactory" by John Pruyn, without funds or a site, no action was taken.

The problems of funds and a site were answered in 1865 when the Legislature appropriated $10,000 for construction and the City of Albany purchased the Congress Hall block and conveyed it to the State.

**First competition design for the new Capitol submitted by
Fuller & Jones in 1863**

As the New Capitol Commissioners—Hamilton Harris, John Pruyn, and Obadiah Latham—began to develop a selection process for the Capitol design, John Pruyn enlisted preeminent New York City architect Richard Morris Hunt to guide the selection process. Hunt was a founding member of the American Institute of Architects and had experience in creating procedures for design competitions. On July 9, 1866, the second design competition was announced, with Hunt's recommendations incorporated.[2]

The New Capitol Commissioners received thirty designs. Thomas Fuller, having entered into a partnership with two Albany architects, submitted a design for the Capitol under the firm name of Fuller, Nichols & Brown. This team set about preparing still another Capitol plan. Fuller may have joined the Albany firm because Nichols and Brown were retained by Senator Ezra Cornell to design his family mansion, Llenroc, on the edge of the university campus in Ithaca.

**Competition design
submitted by Thomas Fuller
and Albany architect
Charles G. Nichols in 1866**

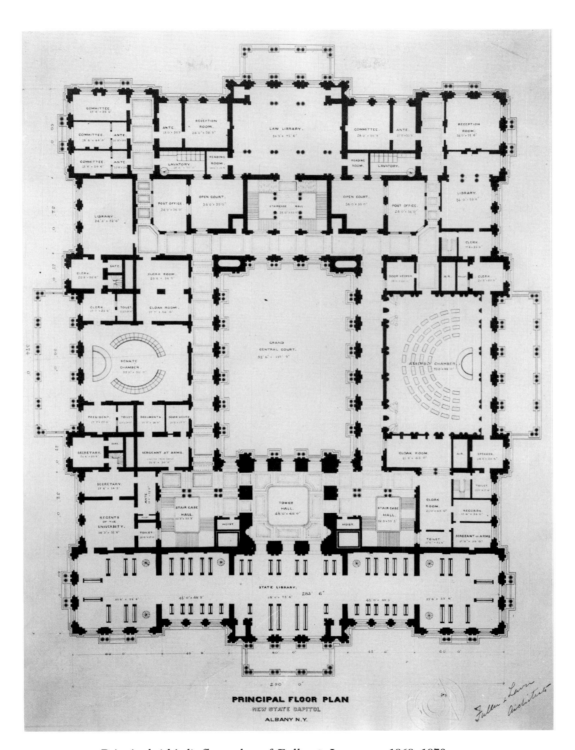

Principal (third) floor plan of Fuller & Laver, ca. 1868–1870

A year slipped away with no significant progress in selecting a Capitol architect. In the interim, Senator Andrew D. White put in a warm recommendation for Arthur D. Gilman as "the best architect in the country for our purposes."[3] White pointed out that Gilman had done many fine buildings in and around Boston, including the city hall, and was just setting up an office in New York. Swayed by White's suggestion, Pruyn looked up Gilman in New York and in May 1867 entertained him as a weekend house guest. Pruyn's hospitality extended to showing Gilman the various Capitol designs previously submitted. Among these was the third design to which Thomas Fuller was a party, this time with his new Albany associates.

On May 13, 1867, the day after Gilman left, the Capitol Commissioners agreed that "no one plan was satisfactory as a whole"[4] but nevertheless announced monetary awards. The firms of Fuller, Nichols & Brown; Schulze & Shoen; and Augustus Laver each received $1,000; Walter Dickson and Harrison & Salter were awarded $750 each; and E. Boyden & Son and Wilcox & King $500 each. The commissioners then authorized Pruyn to contract with Gilman "to prepare a design and plans in conformity with the instructions of the Board."[5] During the summer of 1867 Gilman returned to Albany with an assistant, Edward H. Kendall, and set to work on a detailed scheme for the first and second floors. Pruyn observed that the drawings were progressing in a satisfactory manner. Pruyn later claimed to have proposed an open central courtyard, which Gilman incorporated into his plan. On this and other points Pruyn soon found himself at odds with his fellow commissioners. In fact he was irked to find that Harris, the chairman, was now favoring the newest plans of Fuller, Nichols & Company.

The Legislature stipulated that any design adopted by the New Capitol Commissioners must have the approval of the Commissioners of the Land Office, the lieutenant governor, the attorney general, the secretary of state, and the speaker of the Assembly. The attorney general stoutly insisted that this Capitol must have a dome or a tower on top; as his colleagues were inclined to follow his lead, this issue became paramount. Pruyn viewed the dome idea with distaste, saying it would be "fatal to the project of a large open inner quadrangle which I considered to be one of the marked features of Mr. Gilman's plan."[6] Pruyn and his supporters (Comptroller Thomas Hillhouse and State Treasurer Joseph Howland) did not prevail. After considerable debate the Land Commissioners voted that "in the judgment of the Board, the plan for the new Capitol should include a central dome after the general style adopted in the plans presented by Architect Fuller."[7]

Gilman made an overture to Charles G. Nichols, proposing that they pool ideas. On August 8, Fuller and Gilman were introduced. Gilman was afterward quoted as saying that he merely wished his name to be connected with the Capitol and was willing to leave details to Fuller. On August 14 the New Capitol Commissioners authorized Fuller and Gilman to prepare jointly a new design that reflected the desires of the Commissioners of the Land Office.

While these two rivals had now been harnessed as a team, their partnership was an uneasy one at best. As Gilman explained during later Senate Finance Committee hearings, "My practice is mostly in the Italian Renaissance School," while Fuller thought that the Capitol "ought to be in the Gothic style." "I have no personal hostility to Mr. Fuller carrying out his Gothic architecture," Gilman commented, "but not on my own renaissance design."[8] Meanwhile, a new design by Schulze & Schoen, a New York firm, was picking up support.

John Pruyn—the most actively involved of the Capitol's promoters—made an impromptu railroad journey to Ottawa that November to see Fuller's Parliament building for himself; he also attended the opening ceremonies of the first Parliament elected under the new Dominion of Canada. He was guided around the buildings by Augustus Laver, Fuller's partner, and judged the Gothic structures "better than I had expected to find them. They seem to be very well arranged and constructed."[9]

After Pruyn's return, the New Capitol Commissioners submitted the joint plan of Fuller and Gilman to the Land Office commissioners, who concurred on its approval. That collaboration produced two major results. One was a compromise whereby the open central court was retained, along with the tower, by moving it 50 feet forward, making its weighty substructure serve

Approved design submitted by Thomas Fuller and Arthur D. Gilman, 1867

as the eastern wall of the inner courtyard. The other result was that Fuller agreed with Gilman to treat the exterior in a style that was basically Italian Renaissance. They came up with a massive design crowned by a truly spectacular tower.

Governor Fenton approved the design on December 7, 1867, but the Land Office commissioners waited until the legislators returned to Albany before approving construction. In a speech before the Senate on February 13, 1868, and at an earlier hearing, Obidiah Latham charged that the design details were incomplete, making it impossible to develop an accurate estimate of the cost of the work. The Fuller plans, Latham said, were "not the best that were offered"; they were

> unsuitable and imperfect in important and essential particulars. The leading idea of the arrangement of the interior seems to have been to secure a quadrangle, or open court yard, with a corridor surrounding it. This arrangement destroys the direct communications of the different departments.[10]

The plan, he continued, deprived the building of what any Capitol was normally expected to have—"a grand central hall or vestibule." The external design showed "a want of harmony, and gives the effect of eight distinct buildings." Latham charged that his two fellow commissioners, Harris and Pruyn, were "proceeding with the building without consulting me." And he predicted rightly that the ultimate cost would "far exceed the sum limited in the statute for the completion of the work."[11]

The Senate Finance Committee held a hearing to assess Latham's allegations. The result was that the Legislature in 1868 appropriated another $250,000 to proceed with the building as planned and authorized making it even bigger by the acquisition of more property—an extra half block on the west side of Hawk Street. At the same time, the Legislature cautioned the Capitol Commissioners not to proceed any further if the cost would exceed $4 million. In a move obviously intended to put a damper on Latham's captiousness, the Legislature enlarged the membership of the Capitol Commission from three to eight. This statute took effect on June 8, 1868.

Thomas Fuller ceased his relationship with the Albany firm of Nichols & Brown, summoned Augustus Laver back from Ottawa, and set up the office of Fuller & Laver at 45 North Pearl Street in Albany. The partners took a house together across the river in Greenbush (now Rensselaer). When they won the competition to design the San Francisco City Hall in 1870, Laver moved to the West Coast to carry on that project, while Fuller took full charge of the Capitol. The excavation contract for the Capitol was given to John Bridgford, a local mason and builder, who became the first building superintendent.

The Fuller-Gilman design, being primarily Italian Renaissance in style, did not imitate the Canadian Parliament structures. There were, however, some elements of similarity in their skylines and turrets with fancy iron cresting atop their roofs. What Fuller thought about the Albany building is revealed in his first report to the commissioners:

> In the exterior composition of the design there is a general adherence to the style of the pavillions [sic] of the New Louvre, of the Hotel de Ville of Paris, and the elegant Hall or Maison de Commerce recently erected in the city of Lyons. Without servile imitation of any particular example, the architects have produced a composition in the bold and effective spirit which marks the most admired specimens of modern civil architecture.[12]

The design was a conventional compilation, but it was what State officials and commissioners of the moment desired. The Land Office men had dictated the grandiose tower. Legislators had indicated where they wanted their chambers to be. High-ceilinged rooms were much in vogue. The architects had to please many masters, and Fuller showed himself amenable to changes as the work progressed. When the time came that he had to defend what he had been required to do, he was at least partially justified, it seems, in protesting: "I cannot but express my surprise that the report of the 'advisory board' should place upon me the entire responsibility of the adoption of the central court, the position of the main tower, legislative halls, the size of the rooms, etc., whereas they were called for by those in authority."[13]

The transiency of State officials was a disturbing factor from the start. Plans approved by one year's authorities might be disapproved by the next. Appropriations often were reduced.

On August 12, 1868, the Capitol Commissioners appointed Fuller as Architect of the Capitol at a salary of $10,000 per year. It was then customary for an architect to take as his fee a percentage of the construction cost of the building. When the Commission cannily proposed that he instead accept an annual salary of $10,000, Fuller put up a strong argument but finally acquiesced. Had he been paid a percentage, it was estimated that Fuller would have easily received $250,000 by the time he was dismissed.

In 1869 Arthur D. Gilman assigned to Fuller & Laver the rights to all plans in which he had participated and withdrew to his own thriving practice in New York and Boston.

Thomas Fuller

Foundations of the new Capitol, with cupola and statue of Themis in the background, 1870

CHAPTER FOUR

CORNERSTONE IN THE RAIN

Governor John T. Hoffman

IF THOSE REPRESENTATIVES OF THE PEOPLE APPEARED SINGULARLY UNWORRIED by the ample warnings about the Capitol's construction cost, it must be remembered that—in spite of the depression of the 1870s that quickly ensued—this was a financially freewheeling era. The birth of the Capitol coincided exactly with the rise of the notorious Tweed Ring, and William M. "Boss" Tweed was a member of the State Senate. The scandals of the Grant administration were soon to unfold. Even as the foundations were being laid, Jay Gould and James "Diamond Jim" Fisk precipitated Black Friday with their plot to corner the nation's gold market.

Tweed, the leader of Tammany Hall who had been elected to the Senate in 1867, intended to gain control of the state government. In a lavish suite in an Albany hotel, he "held court" and dispensed his favors to lawmakers who were obedient to him. In 1868, with the help of gross election frauds, he promoted his New York mayor, John T. Hoffman, to the governorship. Political ethics hit rock bottom in Albany. A Tweed biographer has said that "A more degraded Assembly than the one over which Tweed's Speaker presided is hard to conceive. There have been others more corrupt. But this one was without shame."[1]

This was the noxious political atmosphere amid which the Capitol project was undertaken. That Tweed tried to get his fingers into the Capitol pie was strongly insinuated by John V. L. Pruyn at a later date when he had been dropped as a commissioner. "I was left off the Commission by Mr. Tweed," he was quoted in an interview, "for the reason, perhaps, that I was not sufficiently flexible for certain purposes."[2]

In any case, it is perfectly clear that the Legislature authorized construction to proceed. It was common knowledge that the $4 million cost limitation was not to be enforced. When an Assembly subcommittee investigated the skyrocketing cost in 1874, it absolved the commissioners of any blame. The commissioners had given their opinion that the cost would ultimately exceed $10 million. After hearing this, according to the Assembly committee's report, "the Legislature itself assumed all the responsibility for the plans of the building, and adopted the same definitely."[3]

The construction operation began with a prodigious digging, after many buildings were razed. Earth was removed by manual labor to an average depth of more than fifteen feet over an

area of nearly three acres. It was "an extraordinary spectacle"—a continuous procession of two hundred wagons "in close rank from morning to night," carting away the dirt and using it as fill in nearby ravines.

The digging uncovered something that would persist in Capitol legend all down the years—quicksand. The site is underlaid by a deep deposit of glacial lake clay. Laced through the clay were many very fine veins of silt, which, when saturated with water, behaved like quicksand. In each case the disturbed silt and clay was removed and replaced with clay or concrete, according to construction reports to the Legislature. But the specter of quicksand continued to haunt the Capitol.

The initial thought of building entirely with native New York State stone was impractical, but a small granite quarry near Saratoga Springs could supply enough for the foundations and basement. This granite was dark-hued and not of uniform quality. Dr. James Hall, the state geologist, was enlisted to obtain granite samples. On July 7, 1869, the first foundation stone was laid by John V. L. Pruyn. However, a newspaper article stated that the stone was not granite but "a massive limestone from the quarries on the shore of Lake Chaplain."[4] The 1869 *Report of the New Capitol Commissioners* noted that the Saratoga quarry, the only source of granite in the state, had been exhausted. Bids were sought again for the footing and sub-basement stone. By the close of 1869, a total of 9,063 cubic yards of granite and limestone had been delivered from Lake Champlain, Mohawk Valley, and Kingston, New York, quarries.

John McAlpine, the state engineer, devised a support system that took into account the glacial lake clay and the proposed building design. First, the excavated area was blanketed with a six-inch thickness of gravel. Then a three-foot slab of concrete was laid on top of the gravel as a means of equalizing the pressure on the substrate. Finally, a deep, impervious "puddle wall" was built around the entire foundation to exclude water seepage. For centuries this type of support system had been used in medieval Gothic cathedrals that had similarly concentrated, unequal loading.

Granite blocks for the foundations being lifted into place, 1870, *left*

Foundations being laid, 1869

While the Saratoga granite (actually a dark granite gneiss) was being laid for the basement walls, a group of the Capitol commissioners, including Pruyn, made a tour of several quarries in New Hampshire and Maine. They selected granite from Keene, New Hampshire, and Hallowell, Maine, because of its light hue and even texture. Most of the granite for the exterior walls and stairs came from Hallowell; those quarries were close to the coastline, so the granite could be cheaply transported by water.

The commission leased wharves of its own at the Albany waterfront to receive the granite. It contracted with the Albany Railway Company, owner of the local horsecar lines, to haul the stone up the hill. A rail spur was run into the Capitol grounds. For many years, a familiar sight in Albany was the teams of draft horses, hitched in tandem, straining to draw a weighty block of granite on a flatcar up the stiff grade. The company kept three or four standby teams to relieve exhausted horses.

Iron was not an important constituent in the earlier phases of erecting the Capitol. Structural steel was a thing of the future. The solid brick arches of the basement are illustrative of the

Interior courtyard walls under construction, 1873

Beginning of construction of the interior walls, 1873

building's masonry load-bearing construction. The Capitol spanned a transition period in construction practice. Only in the upper portions does one encounter steel. As the Capitol was being completed, skyscrapers were rising in Chicago and New York.

The building became a major industry for Albany. As the Legislature authorized major construction appropriations, the labor force fluctuated between 1,000 and 1,500 men. In 1880, for instance, 1,398 workers, of whom 536 were stonecutters, completed the south section of the building. Cynics often referred to the project as a "patronage factory." There is little question that politics influenced the dispensing of jobs.

When the basement walls had risen to twenty feet, it came time to lay the cornerstone. This event occurred on June 24, 1871. The weather itself provided an omen of things to come. It rained all day.

The cornerstone was prepared several days in advance of the ceremony and laid at the northeast (Washington Avenue) corner of the foundations, which were floored over with planking. Debris was cleared away. The steam engine and crane for hoisting the block of granite into place were neatly painted. A "grand arch" was erected at the east side to serve as an entrance gate for the hundreds of uniformed Masons who were to parade through the

city streets, accompanied by a squadron of cavalry and several brass bands. The arch was decked with evergreens and banners. A steamboat was chartered to bring delegations from Masonic lodges in the Hudson Valley, while others, including the colorful Knights Templar, swarmed into town from across the state.

A cavity had been drilled into the cornerstone to receive mementos of the occasion. They were deposited in a hermetically sealed glass case, which in turn was enclosed in a copper box. This cavity was kept filled with ice water in the interim. It was a brief fad among the townspeople to go uphill and take a drink out of the stone and to toss "lucky coins into the water." A young man stood beside the stone with two dippers and ladled up the innocent brew.

Cornerstone day was to have been a gala day in Albany. Thousands made long journeys to attend. The city awakened to a cold, dismal rain. By 8 a.m. the drizzle settled into a heavy, steady downpour. From the doorways of their hotel headquarters, Knights Templar, in full regalia with cocked hats and white ostrich plumes, peered out disconsolately. Postponements of the long procession were repeated from hour to hour. Finally, orders were given to start the parade at noon, drastically curtailing the scheduled route; many marched under the "unpicturesque cover of a forest of umbrellas." A large crowd defied the rain to line the curbs and throng around the foundations. One bystander was reminded of "marching toadstools." A youth who went home and wrote down his impressions for posterity said, "The American flag endeavored to wave, as is its custom, but being wet with the rain it could only droop around the mast."[5]

Governor John T. Hoffman had the distinction of occupying a portion of Congress Hall as the "Executive Mansion" during his two terms in office (1868–1872). Adam Blake had incorporated the brick dwelling on Park Place nearest the Capitol into the hotel and under legislative authority had it fitted up especially to serve as the governor's residence. Blake expended $30,750 of his own funds on the task, for which he was eventually reimbursed. Hence, Governor Hoffman did not have far to go to officiate at the cornerstone ceremony, and his wife, with other women, was able to watch from the windows.

The governor, trying hard to live down his Tweed background, performed his role with aplomb, despite the fact he had recently proposed that work on the Capitol be suspended while plans were modified in the interest of economy. Hoffman had even suggested that some of the "abundant space" might be used for the official residence of the governor.[6]

Cornerstone being laid in the rain, June 24, 1871

Thomas Fuller, the architect, was on hand to be honored for his work. While the multitudes got drenched, the governor and other main participants had the shelter of canvas awnings on the platform.

Hamilton Harris, the Commission chairman, presided. Governor Hoffman confined his remarks to the history that had led up to the construction, starting with Henry Hudson. He concluded on a platitudinous note: "Let us lay the corner stone of our new Capitol with the prayer that our beloved State may continue to grow in the future as it has in the past."[7]

A workman kept sopping rain out of the cornerstone cavity with a sponge. The governor lowered the metal box into it. Among the contents were copies of all legislation relating to the new Capitol, an 1871 Albany city directory, various U.S. coins and currency of 1871 mintage, and Albany newspapers of the prior day.

Finally, the Masonic order took over. Thomas Fuller was presented to the Grand Master, who handed him a square, level, plumb, and span and read a traditional Masonic prayer to the twenty thousand people in attendance.

Oddly enough, the cornerstone so solemnly laid that rainy day cannot be found today. It was unmarked.

Construction went into full swing. But there was a threat looming for Thomas Fuller.

Completed basement piers, 1870

First-story exterior wall along Washington Avenue, 1871

First-story exterior wall along Washington Avenue, 1873

East facade

CHAPTER FIVE

BATTLE OF THE STYLES

Lieutenant Governor William Dorsheimer

SOMEONE ASKED LEOPOLD EIDLITZ "WHAT BUSINESS" HE HAD TO GRAFT A Romanesque type of architecture upon Thomas Fuller's Italian Renaissance. "What business," Eidlitz countered, "had Fuller to put that basement under my building?"[1]

Leopold Eidlitz was one of two eminent American architects who were contracted to alter the design of the Capitol and see it through to completion after Thomas Fuller was dismissed in 1876. The other was Henry Hobson Richardson.

Eidlitz's barbed witticism suggests the architectural crisis that arose when—after the Capitol was eight years along and going into its third story—a decision was made to change architects. The immediate backfire was a hot debate that flared up in the architectural profession, spread through the public press, and was referred to as the "Battle of the Styles."

Clamor against the building had grown strident. Hostility to its ballooning cost and lengthy delays spilled over into attacks on its design. More and more, it was being disparaged as a "white elephant." The $4 million barrier was breached by 1874. Fuller's estimate now was that it would require $8 million more.

The Capitol was a scapegoat for political inquiries. The Senate Finance Committee, after an 1874 study, concluded that the system under which the work had been done was "not a wise one." The job ought to be "in the hands of one responsible man, who should be a practical builder of large experience."[2] Such a man was James W. Eaton, an Albany building contractor. Governor John A. Dix named him superintendent of construction. Efficiency picked up, but the hue and cry did not subside. Responsible persons felt that

something else was radically wrong. What could it be if not the basic design?

Samuel J. Tilden, popular because of his fight to smash the Tweed Ring, won the governorship in 1875. Along with him, as lieutenant governor, came William Dorsheimer, a Buffalo attorney and a patron of the arts who had founded the Fine Arts

Model of the Fuller and Gilman design, from
The American Architect and Building News, April 15, 1876

Academy and the Buffalo Historical Society. Reform being their watchword, this team was expected to "do something" about the new Capitol. What they did was, in fact, sensational.

The Capitol Commission had been boosted to eight members, none of whom knew much about construction. In 1875, the Legislature abolished the commission and appointed a new board made up of the lieutenant governor as chairman, the attorney general, and the auditor of the Canal Department. Thus, Dorsheimer was handed a unique opportunity to work his will on the partly finished building and to leave behind a lingering controversy.

Dorsheimer's Capitol Commission was required to approve "full detail plans and specifications" of the third floor before more than $50,000 of new appropriations could be spent. In addition, the legislation mandated that no more than half of the appropriation could be expended until plans and specifications for the remainder of the building had been completed and approved. Fuller could not guarantee that he could produce completed plans by December, and this situation had the potential to cause another work stoppage.

No one had given the Fuller plan a critical examination since the work began. Dorsheimer now did so and thought that there must be some better way to complete the building. It was evident that Fuller's mind had been mainly on the exterior and that he had done little toward giving the interior much refinement.

As construction proceeded on the third floor level, awkward features became evident, among them the "great distances to be traversed in passing from one part to another, the height of the less important stories, the length and gloominess of its halls and the unnecessary spaciousness of some apartments for the purposes to which they were assigned."[3] In planning the ceremonial spaces on the third floor, Fuller oriented seating in the Assembly to the north, directly into the glare of the windows. The ceilings of both legislative chambers were to be undistinguished, made of flat cast-iron panels.

The Dorsheimer commission approached its problem in much the way a family physician might treat a patient who was gravely ill: it called in specialists for consultation. It engaged an advisory board of three members. Two of these were top-rank

Leopold Eidlitz

Henry Hobson Richardson

Frederick Law Olmsted

architects, Leopold Eidlitz and Henry Hobson Richardson. The third was the best-known landscape architect of his day, Frederick Law Olmsted, designer of Manhattan's Central Park. The commissioners wanted the third advisor to have "references to the administration, management and economy of public works ruled by aesthetic considerations, than simply as an architectural designer."[4] Olmsted fit the bill.

Dorsheimer knew both Olmsted and Richardson from their work on Buffalo projects. Olmsted had designed the Buffalo park system and collaborated with Richardson on the Buffalo State Hospital. Richardson's commissions also included a house for Dorsheimer and a memorial arch for Niagara Square. Eidlitz had strong ties with New York City Democrats and was a close friend of Montgomery Schuyler, the architectural critic for the *New York World*. The paper's editor, Manton Marble, was a strong supporter of Tilden and a friend to Dorsheimer. It would be through these circles that the advisory board was created in July 1875.

The advisory board was asked to analyze the construction, potential cost savings, improvements to the interior plan, and "all questions of taste and judgment which may suggest themselves as practical consequences to be now discussed."[5] This broad directive opened the investigation into Fuller's basic design. A challenge to a work in progress was highly unusual during these years.

It was a difficult task that was handed these three men—to pick apart the work of a professional contemporary. The defects were not hard to find, but the cure was another thing. The only real cure, one writer remarked, would have been "the heroic remedy of dynamite." The *New York Daily Tribune* diagnosed the case as follows:

> The thing was thrown like a bone to competitors, and was snatched up and carried off by a sturdy builder innocent of any knowledge of the first principles of architecture, and backed by an army of greedy contractors. The sole aim of the design offered was to make a stunning show, to out-Herod Herod with tawdry magnificence on the outside and to let the comfort and convenience, nay the absolute necessities of the business of the legislators and judges for whose sole use the building was intended, go hang.[6]

The report of the advisory board, written by Olmsted, was delivered to the Senate on March 3, 1876. At the outset were compliments for Fuller's design: "We know of no structure for civic purposes of modern times in which regard for stability and endurance is better evinced." But the foundations were worthy of a better-conceived building, commensurate with "the grandeur of the Empire State."[7]

The existing building, the advisory board said, simply lacked "repose and dignity." They enumerated what they considered its many flaws. The upper walls did not suggest the importance of the legislative chambers they were to contain and ought to be "more elegantly formed, richer in detail." The roof had "too much outrigging and top hamper." The board would accept the tower, but wished to modify its shape. By no possibility could the required accommodations of the Capitol "be conveniently arranged on the ground plan of the present building," a plan that could not be rectified without starting over. The central open court was a prime stumbling block. The board bore down upon the location of the Senate and Assembly chambers on the third floor ("as remote from the entrances as they could well be"), and this was another fault it was too late to correct. There was "waste space" everywhere. In place of an unimpressive flight of front steps planned by Fuller, the members proposed a semicircular "advanced terrace" formed of a series of vaulted arches, with a mosaic-tile floor. The reasoning was that the Capitol stood on a slope and that the jutting terrace would counteract the feeling that it was "in danger of sliding down the steep grade."[8]

Sketches proposing alternative solutions to transform the upper stories and roof were attached, but they were never intended to be final designs. The Capitol Commission adopted the recommendations promptly and informed the Senate, in a glow of optimism, that the building could now be finished for an additional $4.5 million (except for the tower and approaches) and that it could be fully completed and ready for occupancy by January 1, 1879.

Preliminary design developed by the Advisory Board for the Capitol, from *The American Architect and Building News*, March 11, 1876

Thomas Fuller was dismissed as of July 1, 1876. He kept the office of Fuller & Laver in Albany for five more years, while listing his home successively at Lake George and Burlington, Vermont. Then he returned to Ottawa and rounded out his life as dominion architect of Canada. He died in 1898, just as the final touches were being put on the Albany Capitol.

The three advisors were appointed as joint architects of the Capitol on September 1, 1876. Though each maintained his separate practice, they organized a firm to carry on the Albany work—Eidlitz, Richardson & Company. Olmsted was its treasurer.

Already, the storm of controversy was raging, triggered by publication of the Eidlitz-Richardson sketches in the March 11, 1876, issue of the *American Architect and Building News,* a new Boston weekly that would become a voice for many East Coast architects. The sketches not only presented "a very decided remodeling of the design above the third floor"; they were accompanied with cost estimates to complete the Capitol.[9]

Before long, the journal was embroiled in a national debate on the merits of the building's design and the role of the advisory board. The editor, W. P. P. Longfellow (a nephew of the poet), wrote that "We doubt if any occurrence in this generation has done more to weaken the general confidence in architects as architects than this unlucky quarrel."[10]

Richard Morris Hunt

The pictures clearly showed a Romanesque style superimposed upon Italian Renaissance. To most architects, such a forced marriage of two distinct classes of architecture was rank heresy. Romanesque was earlier than Renaissance, having arisen out of the fall of the Roman Empire. When civilization bestirred itself again, it found the ruins of Roman structures scattered about western Europe. Awakening architects adopted the arches and vaults of the Roman engineers but made a real art of these

forms, and this was Romanesque. Gothic and Renaissance styles had superseded it, and Romanesque had been neglected for centuries. Then Richardson, thirsting for fresh inspiration, turned back to Romanesque, adding what came to be known as the "Richardsonian touch." And this is how Romanesque crept into the New York Capitol.

During the late nineteenth century the proper use of stylistic elements was an essential component of architectural practice. For this emerging profession, according to architectural critic Montgomery Schuyler, "knowledge of styles was the sum of professional knowledge, and the grammatical putting together of forms of the same period and school was the highest achievement."[11]

Richardson and Eidlitz felt they could make a transition between the two styles that would not be too jarring. They wondered, as Olmsted put it, if "the sap of one style can flow into the other."[12] Distressed at the criticism of so many of their fellow architects, Richardson and Eidlitz always considered that what they did was not so much a question of reconciling clashing styles as of taking a wholly bad building and making it partly good.

There were formal remonstrances to the Legislature and outraged letters to newspapers and periodicals. The most stinging came from the New York Chapter of the American Institute of Architects (of which Eidlitz was a founder and Richardson was a member). It was in the form of a remonstrance to the Senate, signed by the chapter president, Richard Morris Hunt, an old adversary of Olmsted and Eidlitz. "The chapter finds," Hunt wrote, "that the projected work is designed in direct antagonism to the received rules of art. It finds that Italian Renaissance under-stories are surmounted by other absolutely inharmonious Romanesque stories; that no successful attempt has been made to avoid the abrupt transition from one style to the other. The "chapter most respectfully prays," he continued, "that you will not, by causing the construction of this design, establish a great public example which will stand for ages, in all its grandeur of proportion and magnificence of material, to vitiate public taste by its extreme incongruities of form and ornamentation."[13] If the existing structure was so bad as all that, the chapter suggested, it might better be taken down and commenced anew.

Fuller spoke up in his own behalf with a communication to the Senate, rejecting the criticisms of the advisory board point by point and insisting that the grafting of a different style "on a building so far advanced, would present a most unsightly appearance." Many of the features criticized by the advisory board had been added at the request of the New Capitol Commission and were not in Fuller's original design. As president of the local chapter of the A.I.A., Fuller sent copies of his testimony to chapters across the country. Responses from Chicago, Rhode Island, Cincinnati, and Albany were read to the Senate. Governor Tilden held himself aloof from the seething argument. His only recorded comment on the new design was, "How much will it save?"[14]

Nevertheless, no American architect ever before had had such a glittering opportunity as was afforded Eidlitz and Richardson. With Lieutenant Governor Dorsheimer as their powerful champion, they were given tremendous freedom. Dorsheimer's view was that the building should be "a school of architecture in itself to the people of the State."[15] There is a hint, however, in a letter of Olmsted's, that the lieutenant governor kept their exuberance in check: "Dorsheimer, though yielding to professional judgment in the end, has from the first stood in the attitude of remonstrance and resistance to what he has designated as the 'over-sumptuous' inclinations both of Eidlitz and Richardson."[16]

The two architects had not previously been associated. They were wise to divide the interior of the Capitol between them. In a general way, Eidlitz took the Assembly (north) side, Richardson the Senate (south) side. Eidlitz designed the Assembly Chamber, the Assembly and Senate staircases, the Golden Corridor, the tower, the inner courtyard, and the first Court of Appeals courtroom. Richardson worked on the Senate Chamber, the Executive Chamber, the lieutenant governor's office, the Great Western Staircase, and the second Court of Appeals courtroom, as well as on the exterior. Each left the stamp of his personality indelibly upon the building.

Leopold Eidlitz was born in Prague in 1823 and trained at the Vienna Polytechnic Institute. After emigrating to America, he entered the New York City architectural office of Richard Upjohn. Eidlitz designed many important ecclesiastical works, such as Temple Emanu-El (1868) and the Church of the Holy Trinity (1883) in New York and Christ Church Cathedral (1859–1867) in St. Louis. Among his notable commercial and public buildings were the American Exchange Bank (1857), the New York Produce Exchange (1860), and the south wing of the New York County Courthouse (1870s), now known as Tweed Courthouse. He was known for his extensive use of ornament and color, as well as form and structure.

Henry Hobson Richardson was born in Louisiana in 1838, attended Harvard, and studied at the École des Beaux Arts in Paris. After the Civil War he formed a partnership with Charles Gambrill in New York City. The firm was recognized for its planning and design of religious, residential, commercial, and public buildings. His residential commissions—such as the Watts Sherman House (1874) in Newport and later the Hay-Adams House (1884–86) in Washington, D.C., and the Glessner House (1885–87) in Chicago—received critical acclaim in professional journals. Trinity Church (1877) in Boston and later commercial projects such as the Marshall Field Warehouse (1885–87) and the Ames Building (1882–83) in Chicago, along with numerous railroad station commissions and furniture designs, demonstrated the breath of his capabilities. William Dorsheimer selected Richardson for two Buffalo projects—the state hospital complex and his own house.

Eidlitz, Richardson & Company went ahead while the "Battle of the Styles" dinned in their ears. They began by taking down some courses of Fuller's stonework above the second floor. They had worked out modifications that made the transitional third story less jolting than it had seemed in the preliminary sketches. When the facade of this story was done, Eidlitz interposed a belt course of deeply incised arabesque work, which announces that from here on, this building was designed by Eidlitz and Richardson.

**Transition between Fuller's Italian Renaissance and
Eidlitz's and Richardson's Romanesque**

While the architects made only a few attempts to defend their alterations, they were by no means insensitive to the criticisms. Olmsted revealed their "annoyance and worry" in a brisk correspondence he carried on with Charles Eliot Norton, professor of the history of art at Harvard. Norton indicated his sympathy: "I can well understand what a difficult and ungrateful task you have had in trying to get this building into shape."[17] Toward the end of 1876, Olmsted wrote more calmly to Norton:

> The design of the Capitol has since last winter grown more Romanesque but also, I hope, a little more quiet and coherent. There will be much historical incongruity

in it and some that I would gladly have escaped. But we must take men as we find them and Eidlitz would not if he could have it otherwise. If he had been a man who could and would, we might have more weak and meaningless and pottering work, and it is a comfort that we are likely to escape that.[18]

Not surprisingly, the debate about the Capitol reverberated into the 1877 legislative session, and the upshot was another inquiry. Fuller orchestrated an offensive by submitting a new remonstrance signed by more than fifty prominent citizens calling for a return to his original design. As the debate exploded into the popular press, newspapers took sides. The *New York Times* criticized the desire for stylistic purity: "if a Romanesque second story is put upon a Renaissance first story, eruptions of Vesuvius and Helca, earthquakes in California and Calabria, cholera in India, and a low moral tone among Spitz dogs will sooner or later follow."[19] The *Report of a Majority of the Senate Finance Committee* strongly reflected the viewpoint of hostile architects:

> The committee are of the opinion that it was not intended or expected by the Legislature creating the present commission that the style of architecture should be materially changed. The Legislature desired to cheapen the cost of construction if the same was practicable, without lessening the beauty of the structure. . . . To employ two distinct styles of architecture of opposite principles and entirely different in character, on one and the same building or facade, is illogical and incongruous in the extreme, and admits of no defense. . . . Indeed, the folly of attempting to unite the two styles is revolting, not simply to trained professional taste, but to that common sense of harmony which belongs to every eye and mind.[20]

The majority of the Senate Finance Committee finally recommended "that the exterior of the New Capitol be completed in the Renaissance style and in conformity with the original design on which it has thus far been erected."[21] Two members

Leopold Eidlitz's and H. H. Richardson's design, ca. 1877. This was essentially the final design, except for the "advanced terrace" and tower, which were not built.

"North Center," or Assembly side, of the Capitol,
from *Scribner's Monthly*, December 1879

of the five-member Senate Finance Committee dissented in a minority report, insisting that the Commission, by making the change, had in fact "rendered the State service of great value in overcoming glaring defects of portions of the old plan."[22]

Next, astonishingly, the Legislature of the State of New York actually legislated architecture. In making the 1877 appropriation to continue the work, the Legislature attached a rider directing the Commission to "build and complete the exterior of the New Capitol building in the Italian Renaissance style of architecture adopted in the original design, and according to the style upon which the building was being erected prior to the adoption of the so-called 'modified design.'"[23]

Eidlitz and Richardson must have been greatly taken aback—but they managed in a subtle way to have the last laugh. Richardson wrote to their partner, Olmsted, at this juncture, slyly remarking that "I do hope Dorsheimer will be firm, but I do believe *entre nous* that the building can be well finished in Francois 1st or Louis XIV, which come under the head of Renaissance."[24] Thus, rather than working in the style of the Italian Renaissance, Richardson changed signals and designed the roof features in French Renaissance with a decidedly "Richardsonian" flavor. It does not appear that the legislators ever recognized the difference.

Another storm was brewing, in the meantime.

When Governor Samuel J. Tilden ran for the presidency in 1876, his personal choice for a successor at Albany was Lieutenant Governor Dorsheimer. But the Democratic convention, while retaining Dorsheimer as lieutenant governor, nominated Lucius Robinson of Elmira for the governorship. The fact that Dorsheimer openly opposed Robinson's nomination did nothing to sweeten the relationship between these two unlike men after they won the election.

Governor Lucius Robinson, the former state comptroller and an economy-minded man, declared overt war on the Capitol. When the 1877 Legislature passed an appropriation of $1 million to continue work, he vetoed the bill. The veto message was a tirade: "The New Capitol is a great public calamity. . . . It is without a parallel for extravagance and folly. . . . [I]t is more than double the size needed for a Capitol. . . . When this great and useless structure can or will be completed it is idle to conjecture."[25] Robinson's veto ushered in protests from a thousand Capitol workers. Local police were called in to maintain order in the legislative galleries and to guard the governor's mansion.

The Legislature cut the appropriation to $500,000 and passed it by a vote large enough to pass it again over a veto if need be. The governor let it stand. But he did not cease, as long as he was in office, to fulminate against the "public calamity."[26]

The lesser appropriation compelled the Commission to lower its sights. It was impossible to complete the building by January 1, 1879. Instead, it was decided to apply all available funds to finishing up the "North Center" in time for occupancy on that date. The North Center was the section that contained the Assembly Chamber.

During the fall of 1878 the allied architects would travel to Albany on the Hudson River night boat. Usually they were accompanied by Olmsted and sometimes by Lieutenant Governor Dorsheimer. Eidlitz would have a roll of working drawings under his arm, not trusting them out of his sight. Wherever this little group settled on deck, the conversation sparkled. John

Gothic dormers designed by Leopold Eidlitz for walls of the Central Courtyard

Quincy Adams Ward, a noted sculptor who accompanied them, recalled: "There was never so much wit and humor and science and art on that boat before or since."[27]

Leopold Eidlitz-designed dormer with the coat of arms of the Clinton family

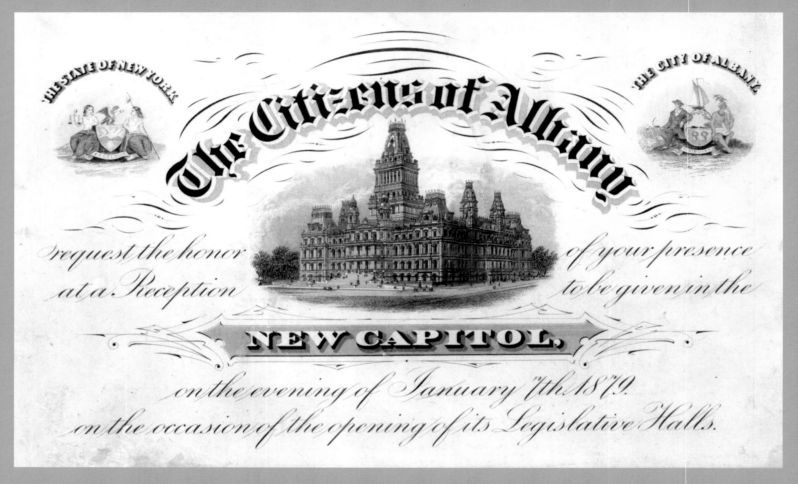

Invitation to the 1879 opening of the Assembly Chamber

CHAPTER SIX

HOUSEWARMING

One of two fireplaces in the Assembly Chamber
designed by Leopold Eidlitz,
below the East Visitors' Gallery

THERE WAS NO HEAT IN THE ASSEMBLY CHAMBER OF THE OLD CAPITOL THAT
cold winter's morning of January 7, 1879. It was not going to be used ever
again. In fact, the chamber had already been stripped of its desks and carpets.

As a matter of form, however, the members of the Assembly came
together, merely to take their farewell of it. They kept their overcoats on
against the chill and stood waiting for the Senate, which was upstairs having
a caucus.

After twenty minutes the worn stairs creaked. The senators came down
in pairs, led by Lieutenant Governor William Dorsheimer and the attorney
general, Augustus Schoonmaker Jr. As the line passed the Assembly door,
the members fell in behind. The procession filed out between the Ionic
pillars, down the familiar tree-lined walk for the last time, and tramped
through the snow from the old Capitol to the completed portion of the
new one.

Washington Avenue was alive with spectators, as this was a big day
for Albany.

At the Washington Avenue entrance of the "North Center" the legislators were welcomed by James W. Eaton, the building superintendent. He
guided them up the Assembly Staircase and into the wondrous Assembly
Chamber. It was the first glimpse most of them had of this room, the fame

of which already was nationwide—"the grandest legislative hall in the world," as some writers described it.[1]

Lieutenant Governor Dorsheimer mounted the rostrum, banged the gavel, and intoned: "The Senate has escorted the Assembly from the old Capitol to the new one. And now, in this presence, I declare the chambers formally transferred to the Legislature. The Senate will now retire to its own room."[2]

The Senate Chamber, however, would not be ready for another two years. In the meantime, the Senate would sit in the oak-paneled courtroom built for the Court of Appeals. This was on the floor below the Assembly, and it opened upon the Golden Corridor. (A quip was heard about the Senate's having become the "Lower House.") The Golden Corridor was an east-west gallery leading from the second floor landing of the Assembly Staircase. Its popular name was derived from the fact that Eidlitz had here indulged his passion for Arabic ornamentation.

The temporary chambers of the governor, also off the Golden Corridor, were to the east of the temporary Senate Chamber. Gov. Lucius Robinson, nevertheless, did not intend to recognize the existence of the new Capitol and refused to deliver his annual message inside its walls. A newspaper reported that "It has been stated that the Governor objects to occupying his new quarters at present, but it is certainly difficult to perceive why he does so, or concede the soundness of his reasons for remaining in his present cramped, uncomfortable and ill-ventilated quarters."[3]

Neither house stayed in session more than an hour that Tuesday. Snow had crippled railroad traffic from the west so that many legislators had been unable to reach Albany. Besides that, who could get down to business when the Capitol was being festively opened? The town was teeming with important visitors, and the Capitol would be the scene of a lavish reception that evening.

Governor Lucius Robinson

The Senate had intended to play host for this reception. Just before adjourning the previous session, each senator had donated $50 to that end. But the citizens of Albany had snatched the ball away from the Senate, deciding it would be more appropriate for them to sponsor the opening. A Society of the Capital was formed and donations solicited. Each $25 subscriber got a ticket of admission for the reception. Invitations went out to four thousand persons of note throughout the state.

The Society of the Capital made the gesture of asking Governor Robinson to do the receiving. Not unexpectedly, he refused. Another invitation related to the event was rebuffed by the governor. The Albany Burgesses Corps, a fashionable drill corps, planned a New Capitol Ball downtown in Martin Hall. Officers of the Burgesses Corps tactfully announced that the governor had declined to attend.

The attitude of the governor explains why the official "receiving" in the governor's temporary office in the new Capitol was performed by the mayor of Albany, Michael Nolan, as chairman of the citizens' committee. Lieutenant Governor Dorsheimer hovered over the affair, mingling with the guests, relishing the plaudits.

Not merely the local press but New York papers described the evening as "the grandest social event in the history of Albany."[4] An endless parade of sleighs moved down Washington Avenue to discharge passengers at the only entrance yet available. Ladies in dazzling gowns, decked with jewels, alighted on the arms of distinguished escorts. Full dress predominated. An estimated eight to ten thousand people attended.

With less than one-fourth of the building open, such a number meant a human traffic jam. Everyone took the grand tour: up the Assembly Staircase, through the Golden Corridor with a detour into the Court of Appeals (Senate Chamber, pro tem), and on up to the pièce de résistance, the Assembly Chamber. The stately stairway was a solid stream of humanity,

Under the East Gallery, *Scribner's Monthly*, December 1879

Court of Appeals, designed by Leopold Eidlitz,
Scribner's Monthly, December 1879

half of it struggling upward and meeting the other half coming back. To be sure, there were elevators; these steam lifts were finished in beautiful carved hardwood.

Part of the plan had been to have dancing in the Golden Corridor, but the crush was so great that it had to be given up. Two popular bands of the era were playing—Austin's Orchestra, from Albany, in the Golden Corridor and Gilmore's Band of New York City on the floor of the Assembly Chamber. They played the quartet from *Rigoletto,* Weber's "Invitation to the Dance," Rossini's overture to *Semiramide,* and Strauss waltzes.

It was as much an architectural as a social occasion. Seldom has an American architect had so triumphant an hour as did Leopold Eidlitz. The interior of the North Center was completely his. Eidlitz stood in the Assembly Chamber, a radiant look on his face. Praises of his work rang in his ears. John Hay, who had been President Abraham Lincoln's secretary, stood near him, gazing at the ceiling, and lauded the architect's work.

The guest list included celebrities such as Edward Everett Hale, author, historian, and clergyman; George W. Curtis, lecturer, journalist, and Chancellor of the State University of New York; David Dudley Field, the noted attorney; and two ex-governors, Horatio Seymour and John T. Hoffman. Special homage was paid to the venerable Thurlow Weed, erstwhile "dictator" of the Whig Party and at 81 the oldest former legislator on the scene.

Eidlitz had done a spectacularly daring thing with the ceiling of his Assembly Chamber. He had given it the widest spanning groined stone arch ever attempted. The keystone of the central vault, which weighed three tons, was 56 feet above the floor. While the chamber was emphatically Gothic in style, it was strongly marked with Eidlitz's penchant for the oriental. The groins of the stone arches were embroidered with incised decoration, colored with vermilion and ultramarine and edged with gold. Upholding the arches were four huge pillars

The restored Assembly Staircase designed by Leopold Eidlitz

Golden Corridor, 1882

Original door hardware in the west corridor, first floor

of polished red granite. In the high lunettes of the north and south walls were the allegorical murals just finished by William Morris Hunt. Rows of stained glass arched transoms were below the murals. The stone walls were carved in intaglio figures, the ground of which was painted vermilion. There were two wonderfully carved stone fireplaces under the galleries, and a blank stone frieze around the walls, which was intended to be carved with historical bas-reliefs by John Quincy Adams Ward. Due to a lack of funding, the carving was never done.

The Golden Corridor was scarcely less adorned than the Assembly Chamber. More than anything else in the Capitol, this hall deserved the term "Alhambresque," and it is one of the vanished splendors. On the second floor it was lighted by the windows of the Central Court. It was 140 feet long, 25 feet wide, 27 feet high, and its "mass of gorgeous color" elicited gasps of admiration. The ceiling, on a smaller scale, was somewhat similar to that of the Assembly Chamber, a series of stone groined arches, with a diaper pattern of blue, red, and umber on a ground of gold. The Golden Corridor lasted little more than a decade.

The Assembly Staircase had not been completely decorated at the grand opening. A *New York Times* article from December 1879 explained that "the walls of the grand staircase, which were last year severely plain, have been colored a warm red brown; the arches of the doors and windows facing the staircase have been touched with lines of gold, and a band of gold, marked

New Assembly Chamber, from *Harper's Weekly*, February 1, 1879

with a conventional floral pattern, in vermillion, extends along the wall about four feet from the floors and the steps. As the visitor climbs the staircase, he finds, on reaching the Assembly floor, that the stone-work has been completed clear to the roof, and that the upper walls are glorious in red and gold, and that a sky-light of stained glass has taken the place of the rude temporary sky-light of last winter."[5]

Eidlitz also had taken as part of his task the finishing of the central courtyard bequeathed by Thomas Fuller. Eidlitz treated it with dormers that are distinctly different from Richardson's dormers on the exterior facades. They have bands of arabesque carving and also carry the finely carved coats of arms of prominent early New York families.

Despite wintry weather, a refreshment tent was set up in the roofless inner court. Mounds of food were supplied by caterers. Patrons found a "cool lunchroom," even though heat was piped into the tent.

Assembly Chamber, designed by Leopold Eidlitz and completed in 1879

Assembly Chamber window, from *Scribner's Monthly*, December 1879

Around 10 o'clock a whisper ran through the jostling throng. The governor was coming, after all. Reluctantly, Governor Robinson had decided it would not do for him to ignore such an occasion altogether. He strode through, escorted by his staff with cocked hats and swords. Robinson remained in the building no more than twenty minutes. A *Times* reporter pictured the governor as seeming to be "annoyed by the scene; that he was offering himself as a sacrifice merely because he knew that duty demanded his presence, and that all the time not a fibre of his being responded to all the splendor and the rejoicing."[6]

The public housewarming was well received, and legislators attended. But it did not cover all the initiation that the lawmakers felt to be the just due of the new Capitol. Acting on the suggestion of Senator Ira Harris, the Legislature scheduled a formal ceremony of its own for the evening of February 12, to take place in the Assembly Chamber. Of course, the governor was invited.

Just as the program was about to begin, Lieutenant Governor Dorsheimer cleared his throat and read a communication from Governor Robinson, which said:

> I find, with extreme regret, that I shall be deprived of the privilege of listening to the addresses of yourself, Speaker Alvord and Mr. Brooks, this evening as I had hoped to do. Every moment of my time is occupied with official duties of unusual urgency. I see, moreover, by the morning papers, that the ceremonies are expected to occupy three or four hours, and I am advised by my oculist that there would be a great danger of entirely arresting the improvement going on with my eyes if I should expose them to the gas-lights in the Assembly Chamber even for one-fourth of that time, and he protests against it most earnestly.[7]

A handsome big armchair had been provided for the governor to sit in. It stood conspicuously vacant while speeches were made by Speaker Thomas G. Alvord, Assemblyman Erastus

Brooks, and Lieutenant Governor Dorsheimer. The latter concluded by saying: "When our future shall be the past, it must be that those who shall live then will rejoice that the Capitol has been built so strong that its associations and its traditions will endure to the latest generation."[8]

As had been predicted, Governor Robinson obdurately refused to move his office from the old Capitol. When it came time to deliver his message to the Legislature, he sent his secretary over with it. The message was heavy with sarcasm where it touched upon the move:

I sincerely hope that you will find the change conducive to your health and comfort, and in every way so agreeable and convenient that you will not regret it. If the occupation of their new and gorgeous apartments shall lead the two houses of the Legislature to so emulate the exalted virtues which have, at different times and on many occasions, adorned the history of the old chambers, that they shall enact only wise and good laws; that they shall honestly and faithfully execute the great trust committed to them by the people; that they shall strictly obey the Constitution and the laws; that they shall establish and maintain a higher tone of public morality, the enormous cost of the building will be repaid in something better than money. But if, on the other hand, no such effects appear; if the lamentable vices, which have too often marked the legislation of the old building, shall stain that of the new; if the extravagant expenditure made upon it is to stimulate profuse and wasteful appropriations to other objects; if, instead of encouraging a plain and honest republican simplicity, it is to cultivate a weak and vain desire to imitate the manners of European courts or to rival regal magnificence and imperial splendors; nay, more, if bribery and corruption, following naturally in the wake of such influences, shall soil the new chambers, the people will have cause to regret the erection of such a Capitol, and to wish that the earth might open and swallow it up.[9]

Central Courtyard

That autumn a Tammany split in the Democratic Party defeated Robinson for reelection. A Republican, Alonzo B. Cornell, succeeded him.

Governor Robinson restrained his antipathy to the building sufficiently to perform the traditional courtesy of escorting the incoming governor to his inauguration. But his subconscious rejection of it evidently remained. Observers noted that he looked pale and ill as he entered the Assembly Chamber, arm and arm with Mr. Cornell.

Rendering of proposed restoration of the Assembly Chamber; watercolor by Peter Ferber for Mesick, Cohen, Waite Architects

CHAPTER SEVEN

THE VANISHING MURALS

William Morris Hunt, self-portrait

ON DIZZY SCAFFOLDINGS 40 FEET ABOVE THE FLOOR OF THE ASSEMBLY CHAMBER, a frail-looking man with a graying beard wielded brushes during the autumn of 1878. Time pressed upon him, and his strength was hardly adequate to the task, though he did have the help of his assistant, John G. Carter. He was applying oil pigments directly to the bare sandstone in the lunettes on the north and south walls.

The man exulted in the work and said: "I would rather carry out this project than be Governor of the state."[1] To a friend he wrote, "I can tell you it is like sailing a 'seventy-four,' or riding eight horses in a circus. It fills one's lungs to breathe in front of such spaces."[2] He was William Morris Hunt, one of the most important American artists of the nineteenth century. Born in 1829, he attended Harvard but left to study painting in Europe under Thomas Couture and Francois Millet. In 1855, Hunt returned to Boston and became the "most powerful artistic force" in that city.[3] His brother, the architect Richard Morris Hunt, had signed the remonstrance to the State Legislature against changing the architectural style of the Albany Capitol.

While Hunt was working at Niagara Falls in early 1878, William Dorsheimer approached him about a possible commission for the Assembly Chamber. In June of that year Hunt received a letter from Leopold Eidlitz outlining the project: "It is proposed to have some allegorical or legendary paintings in the Assembly Chamber of the new Capitol at Albany. Lieutenant

Governor Dorsheimer thinks that you would be willing to give us some advice, perhaps personal assistance in the matter; and requests that you call at my office to examine a sketch indicating the work to be done, with a view to a proposed engagement."[4]

Hunt went to see Eidlitz, and they took an instant liking to each other. The architect sized Hunt up as "not only an artist, but a philosopher."[5] Hunt was engaged to paint two murals for a fee of $15,000 and was told the Chamber would be in shape for him to start by September—but that the murals must be finished in time for the January 1879 opening of the North Center.

At that moment the political climate of the Capitol was remarkably favorable to the arts. Dorsheimer envisioned the building as not just a seat of government but a shrine of art. Fine paintings should adorn its walls, and sculpture should inhabit its corridors. Hunt found himself instantly at home and said:

"Here I am in my own world, and I want to stay here."[6] In fact, he was virtually promised a continuing contract for future painting in the Capitol and began shaping plans to move to Albany permanently.

In his Boston studio, Hunt went immediately to work on thirty charcoal cartoons, twelve pastel sketches, and seventeen oil studies for the murals. Two themes had been haunting his mind for years, and he had done sketches, models, and figure studies for them over the previous decades. His two murals, *The Discoverer,* personified by Columbus, and *The Flight of the Night,* featuring Anahita, the Persian moon goddess, filled the 40-by-16-foot lunettes. Hunt left no record of the meaning behind the murals, but in 1888 Hunt's widow, Louisa Hunt, provided an interpretation of the murals as "allegorical representations of the great opposing forces which control all nature. . . . They

The Flight of the Night by William Morris Hunt,
on the north wall of the Assembly Chamber

represent Negative and Positive, Night and Day, Feminine and Masculine, Darkness and Light, Superstition and Science, Pagan and Divine Thought."[7] Clarence Cook described the murals in the *New York Tribune*:

> On the north wall is the allegory of Ormuzd and Ahriman, the flight of evil before good, of Night before the Dawn. Night's charioteer on his ebon car is hurled along before the breaking day by three plunging, rearing steeds, who subdue their haughty crests. . . . The goddess leaves the charge of her steeds wholly to the guide. . . . The opposite allegory is of the discoverer who sails out on unknown seas, following the sinking sun and attended by Fortune, who holds the tiller of his mounting bark. Science also unrolls her scroll. Hope,

who points the way, and Faith, who hides her face and lets the waves take her where they will.[8]

While it was known that Hunt had received a copy of the Persian poem *Anahita* from his brother in 1846, it is unclear how the complex symbolism of that goddess and Columbus relate to one another. As art historian Henry Adams noted, "Hunt's murals are perplexing precisely because his symbols are derived from different sources and are of different types. They do not completely harmonize, nor lend themselves to a single mode of interpretation."[9]

Hunt had invented a set of pigments that would dry unusually hard and with a luminous appearance. He ordered samples of the sandstone used in the chamber sent to him and experimented with painting directly on the absorbent stone. Hunt

Cartoon of *The Discoverer* by William Morris Hunt, used for the mural on the south wall of the Assembly Chamber

Assembly Chamber, showing *The Discoverer*, from *Harper's Weekly Magazine*, February 1, 1879

wanted the color of the stone to be part of the artwork and not use an intervening layer such as plaster or canvas. The location of the murals was difficult: they would be very high in the room and poorly lighted. To overcome this, he chose to use strong primary colors and heavy outlines. Hunt's Albany murals and John LaFarge's murals (1879) at Trinity Church in Boston became the harbingers of the American mural movement.

September came, and Hunt was told that the staging could not be ready for him until mid-October. On the night of October 19, Hunt began by casting magic lantern slides of his cartoons on the walls and tracing them to the proper size. Stairs for access were built from the Assembly gallery to the north arch. A wood floor spanned the lunette. An 8-foot-wide bridge connected the north platform to the south lunette and was supported by large wood trusses. Fifteen-foot-high stepladders allowed Hunt and his assistant to reach the entire upper wall. Painting was begun on October 28 and finished on December 23.

While painting, Hunt was enthralled by the bustle of the workmen down below and began to think of a future mural that would illustrate their labor—immortalizing them upon the walls of the very building they were erecting. Nothing pleased him more than when a bricklayer or hod carrier climbed the ladder to make favorable comments on his work. "What a big thing a great building is," he wrote. "People grumble and whine about the money which is 'thrown away' upon it; but I tell you that it is an immense work, and worthy of any state or nation. It is the greatest thing which this state has ever done! and a very sensible way in which to spend money."[10]

Hunt spent time in the studio of Erastus Dow Palmer, which was almost in the shadow of the rising Capitol. Palmer, a sculptor of national note, shared Dorsheimer's dream of making the Capitol a repository of fine art.

Palmer had recently done a statue of Chancellor Robert R. Livingston for the Hall of Statuary in the U.S. Capitol. As his own expense, he made a second cast of it, in the hope that it could be placed in the New York Capitol. With Dorsheimer's help, he finally got the statue into the Golden Corridor, later into the Court of Appeals courtroom. But the State never purchased it, keeping it as a loan, and it finally came to rest in the rear of the present Court of Appeals on Eagle Street.

Another hopeful sculptor during this period was John Quincy Adams Ward, who was to carve historical bas-reliefs for the vacant wall panels of the Assembly Chamber. Limited appropriations cancelled this project. There was some posthumous justice for Ward in the fact that his model for an equestrian statue of General Philip Sheridan, with some finishing touches by Daniel Chester French, was used many years later for the statue of Sheridan that today adorns East Capitol Park.

Augustus Saint-Gaudens was suggested as the sculptor for the bas-relief carving on the fireplace breasts in the Senate Chamber, but fiscal austerity forced cancellation of this project as well.

William Morris Hunt finished his murals, and they stirred almost as much comment as the Chamber itself. Said one art critic, "Nothing as yet undertaken here in the art of monumental decoration at all approaches these mural paintings of Mr. Hunt, in the dignity of the composition as a whole, in the beauty of the parts, in the mastery of the execution."[11]

Plaster model of Chancellor Robert Livingston, by Erastus Dow Palmer

Though thoroughly exhausted from laboring under such pressure, Hunt was in the Chamber the night of the opening reception.

Hunt's hopes for remaining permanently as a Capitol artist were soon dashed. Governor Robinson took an especially dim view of costly murals. The Legislature cut the 1879 appropriation in half and restricted the use of the money to the outside walls and the roof, "without any internal ornamentation."

Hunt returned to Boston weakened and extremely depressed. That summer he accepted an invitation to recuperate in a cottage at the Isles of Shoals off the coast of New Hampshire and Maine, but he died there in September.

Remnants of *The Discoverer* above the Assembly Chamber ceiling

The murals survived their painter by a scant ten years.

The roof gutters of the North Center were made entirely of stone, without metal linings. They began to leak. Water seeped inside the walls and discolored the murals. Patches of paint flaked off.

Then the famous arched ceiling cracked dangerously. The wood and papier-mâché coffered ceiling that replaced it, at a level twenty feet lower, sealed the paintings off from public view. The upper portion of the figures, however, remained above the ceiling in the attic loft from which the Assembly lights and ventilation are operated. There, fragments of *The Discoverer* and *The Flight of Night* survive.

Restored Senate Chamber, designed by H. H. Richardson

CHAPTER EIGHT

RICHARDSON'S LEGACY

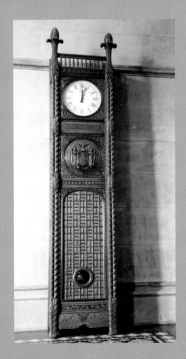

Case clock, designed by H. H. Richardson,
in the Senate Corridor

WHILE THE ASSEMBLY WAS SETTLING INTO ITS DRAMATIC NEW CHAMBER, HENRY Hobson Richardson was designing a magnificent chamber on the Senate side, or the "South Center." Now it was Richardson's turn to make what Goethe called "frozen music."

Governor Alonzo B. Cornell, son of the founder of Cornell University, was as frugal-minded as Lucius Robinson, but a shade more flexible. Cornell had been a member of the Capitol Commission from 1868 to 1871. He had opposed the initial construction because he doubted the Capitol could be built for $4 million. Elected governor in the fall of 1879, Cornell believed that the Capitol was "so far advanced that there seems to be no rational course left but to provide for its completion in the most advantageous manner possible."[1]

The 1880 Legislature loosened the purse strings to the extent of $1.6 million, with the proviso that "the Senate chamber shall be completed and furnished and ready for occupation by the Senate on the 1st day of January, 1881."[2]

Another deadline for an architect to meet. Richardson had more leeway, however, than had been granted to Leopold Eidlitz on the Assembly side. His plans for both the Senate and Executive chambers were well in hand long before there was any roof over the South Center.

In some of the design detail of the Senate Chamber, Richardson had the services of a promising young man who had been an apprentice in his office. This disciple was Stanford White, who would make his own mark as an architect before being shot to death by a jealous Harry K. Thaw.

In May 1878, White confided in his sculptor friend Augustus Saint-Gaudens that he and Richardson had "just tackled the Albany Senate Chamber, and between us cooked up something pretty decent."[3] It may well have been White who suggested having Saint-Gaudens do the sculptures for the Senate chimney pieces, an idea which never materialized.

Although the Capitol's best friend, Lieutenant Governor Dorsheimer, went out of office at just about this time (he later became the federal district attorney for Southern New York),

Senate Chamber, 1881, soon after opening. Today there are double the number of senators.

his influence lingered long enough for Richardson to make his elegant contributions to the interior. The architect was able to lavish such sensitivity and loving care upon the Senate Chamber that *Harper's Weekly* declared that the room "surpasses in magnificence any legislative hall on this continent."[4] By this time, Richardson had moved his offices from New York to Boston.

Even while the Senate Chamber was taking shape, its creator was drawn into the worries of his partner Eidlitz about the Assembly Chamber. The bad omens began almost as soon as it was occupied. The acoustics were atrocious. The magnificent ceiling swallowed sound and tossed echoes. The acoustical defects caused blunders in legislation. An assemblyman voted against his own bill—by mistake. Some bills got so muddled in this way that they were recalled from the governor to save them from veto.

The Assembly took the usual remedial measure: it appointed a committee. The committee took it up with the architects. The architects denied there was any "organic acoustic defect" and blamed the trouble on the freedom of visitors to ramble about the room during session and "indulge in conversation." They suggested raising the Speaker's desk a few inches and moving the seats of members closer together, but there was no improvement.[5]

There was another, more ominous sign. Barely a month before the 1880 Legislature was due to convene, Superintendent James Eaton spotted a fissure in a stone in the rib of an arch overhead.

Eidlitz came hurrying up from New York. The damaged stone was removed, and 60 tons of stone and brick was placed above the arch to relieve unequal pressure. Eidlitz "instituted a theoretical inquiry into the relation of the lines of pressures to the voussoirs of the ribs."[6] He then checked anchorage. Two engineers, R. H. Bingham and William H. Slingerland, were hired to make a study. They reported that some uneven settling may have occurred in the foundations but that it was safe for the Assembly to occupy its chamber.

The Assembly met, albeit with some uneasy glances at the ceiling. No more cracks were in sight. But then the members heard that chinks of masonry were appearing in the Golden Corridor, right beneath them. The whole Assembly took a walk downstairs to see and found the report to be true. After all, such a weighty building did have a lot of settling to do.

Richardson, meanwhile, was composing a symphony of a room. The Senate Chamber is generally regarded as the handsomest room he ever did. He had the same box-like space as Eidlitz with which to contend. Yet he needed much less space to accommodate a legislative body of only thirty-two members. There was little he could do about its height, but he could pull in the walls. This he did by treating the east and west spaces as lobbies, placing the visitors' galleries above them.

Mindful of Eidlitz's acoustical troubles with the Assembly Chamber, Richardson tried nothing adventurous with the Senate ceiling. He left it flat, though of richly carved and deep-paneled oak.

Richardson had an exceptional feeling for the qualities, tones, and textures of building materials and employed them almost as a painter might his pigments. He brought onyx from Mexico, Siena marble from Italy, red granite from Scotland. The onyx paneling of the north and south walls always has been one of the famous features of this exquisite chamber. The ultimate in luxury was attained with red leather and carved mahogany paneling on the walls below the galleries.

Richardson and Eidlitz designed the furniture for their rooms, and some was fabricated on site. The tall, lushly carved presiding chair Richardson made for the lieutenant governor is an extra spacious seat because Dorsheimer, like Richardson himself, was a corpulent person. The architect also designed a few superb tall case clocks, one of which is still the official Senate timepiece, while another stands sedately in the Senate corridor.

While Richardson was working on the Senate Chamber, the city hall of Albany burned down. His involvement with the Capitol led to his engagement to design a new city hall, which he did in a Romanesque style; it was completed in 1881.

Owing to layoffs of laborers and sundry other difficulties, the Senate Chamber did not quite meet its deadline. It was first occupied on March 10, 1881, and it still required some finishing touches.

Upon the opening of the new chamber, the Assembly returned the courtesy of two years before. It escorted the Senate across the building for a formal ceremony. The galleries were

Restored Senate Lobby

jammed. Lieutenant Governor George G. Hoskins presided and boasted of the room that was unquestionably the most beautiful ceremonial space in the nation, if not the world.

Assemblyman James W. Husted of Peekskill closed the ceremonies, exclaiming that "A more magnificent building, a more characteristic structure, does not exist throughout the boundless realms of this universe."[7] Writing in *Frank Leslie's Popular Monthly,* M. E. W. Sherwood, found the Senate Chamber to rival "St. Mark's in Venice in its gorgeous detail" and celebrated the chamber as "the success of the Capitol. Never were senators so nobly lodged. The whole detail is the perfection of modern decorative art."[8]

Richardson finished the Executive Chamber at approximately the same time as the Senate Chamber, Governor Cornell being the first to occupy it, on September 29, 1881. The architect's passion for warm color and luxury also went into this spacious room (60 by 40 feet in plan). He treated its walls with a high wainscot of paneled mahogany and above this with Spanish red leather. The handsome beams of the carved oak ceiling topped it off. Of several spectacular fireplaces in the Capitol, that in the Executive Chamber is one of the best. Governors for a long time actually used this chamber as an office. In late years they have sought the privacy of a smaller adjoining office, and the "Red Room," as it is sometimes called, is used by governors for hearings, press conferences, and ceremonial occasions.

Richardson also designed the lieutenant governor's office, west of the Senate Chamber—a perfect gem of a room, which is purely a working office and is rarely seen by the public.

When the Senate moved into its own chamber, the Court of Appeals courtroom was released to the court for its original purpose. However, the structural failure that plagued the courtroom

Lieutenant Governor's Office

Executive Chamber, designed by H. H. Richardson

**Court of Appeals, designed by H. H. Richardson.
In 1917 the room was moved to State Hall
(the present Court of Appeals building) on Eagle Street.**

caused the judges to request space elsewhere. Governor Cornell told the 1882 Legislature that "The Judges of the Court of Appeals express dissatisfaction with the apartments designed for their use, and seem unwilling to occupy them at present. They desire to have rooms set apart for them in another quarter of the building, and have indicated a preference for a portion of the space originally intended for the State Library."[9]

The substitute courtroom was placed in the southeast corner of the third floor, directly above the Executive Chamber. With this the judiciary was satisfied. The *Albany Evening Journal* praised the suite as "the most magnificent in the building." The new courtroom was touted for its excellent lighting and was considered "far more spacious and elegant."[10] Except for the ceiling and marble window surrounds, this room was moved

intact in 1917 to its present location in the Court of Appeals building on Eagle Street.

Amid the architectural juggling, the State Library—originally planned to extend entirely across the front of the Capitol on the third and fourth floors—was shifted to the same relative position on the west side.

H. H. Richardson died in April 1886, at the age of forty-eight. William Dorsheimer, the former lieutenant governor who had lured him to Albany, paid him this tribute: "There is no painter or sculptor, nor, as we think, any living poet, who has won a reputation so enduring. . . . No one used architectural forms with so much originality, no one with so much grace and tenderness, no one with such strength; nor has any one ever so impressed them with his own personal individuality."[11]

Great Western Staircase, planned by H. H. Richardson and with Isaac Perry responsible for the completed design

CHAPTER NINE

ISAAC PERRY APPOINTED CAPITOL COMMISSIONER

Isaac Perry

THE TELEGRAM CAME AS AN UTTER SURPRISE TO ISAAC PERRY. PUZZLED, HE looked again to be sure he had read the signature correctly. It read Grover Cleveland, Governor. The message said that Governor Cleveland would appreciate it if Perry could come to Albany and see him. Isaac Perry couldn't imagine what for. He never had met Cleveland, and political plums were not his dish.[1]

Perry was past the age of sixty and was prospering as a builder and self-trained architect in Binghamton, New York. Some of the most admired buildings in Binghamton and Elmira were his work. His fellow townspeople respected him, too, for solidity of character. Perry was content where he was.

Still, he did not ignore a summons from the governor. Perry caught a train for Albany, wondering. He was a brawny, big-statured man with a flowing white beard, and the niceties of personal appearance were not one of his worries. The suit in which he went to see the governor was dusty and stood in need of pressing. The hat was a battered, wide-brimmed slouch that he wore daily at work.

The anteroom to the Executive Chamber was full of people. The new governor was creating quite a stir with his "open-door policy." Anyone, within reason, could get in to see him. There was a saying that he might as well set his desk out in front of the Capitol, where he could have the extra advantage of fresh air.

69

Isaac Perry expected to take his turn and have a long wait. But the secretary took a look at his card and ushered him at once into the Chamber, much to the disgruntlement of those ahead. When he departed, the man next in line was admitted and came right to the point. He would like to apply for the newly created post of Commissioner of the Capitol. "As it happens," the governor replied, "I have just now made that appointment."

The applicant's jaw dropped. "What! That farmer-looking man?" "The same." The interview came to an abrupt end.[2]

The reaction of Capitol politicians was much similar. Who was this Perry, they wanted to know. The grapevine had it that a certain man from down the Hudson, politically "deserving," had been slated for the $7,500 position.[3]

Perry went home to prepare his wife for a move that neither of them especially craved. The governor had flung him a challenge he simply could not resist, even though it meant a financial sacrifice. The Capitol had been under construction for fifteen years and was still far from finished. Grover Cleveland wanted him to take sole charge and get it done—hopefully, within three years. The governor's only injunction was to "be as economical as possible . . . but not lose sight of erecting it in a substantial and creditable manner."[4]

The governor, seemingly, had picked Isaac Perry out of nowhere. True, he happened to be a Democrat, but for voting purposes only. He had pulled no wires and in fact did not even know the job had been created. In an era when the Capitol project was cynically called a "patronage factory," such an appointment

was unheard of. Perry handed the politicians another jolt by announcing his employment policy: he would hire men on merit alone and on their ability to deliver a fair day's work, regardless of their politics.

The work had been governed by New Capitol Commissions ever since it started. When Governor Cleveland took office in 1883—elected because of his record as the reform mayor of Buffalo—he found that the cost of the Capitol already had exceeded $14 million and declared that "the building should be finished as quickly as practicable, and the delays, errors and expense attending its construction, if possible, forgotten."[5]

The way to do this, Cleveland believed, was to abolish the hydra-headed commission and substitute a qualified, single Commissioner of the Capitol. A compliant Legislature passed a bill creating such a position, to be filled by "a suitable person who shall be skilled in the construction of buildings and architectural plans." The governor signed it the day it was passed, and at the same time—before any political undertow could get going—sent to the Senate his nomination of Isaac G. Perry, which was confirmed.

Perry had not foreseen the difficulties of a job so subject to political pressures and legislative vagaries—or that it would take another fifteen years to finish the Capitol. James W. Eaton was dismissed as building superintendent when Perry took over.

Governor Cleveland was especially anxious to see the Senate Staircase built without delay. The Assembly Staircase was the only one as yet completed.

Perry started the Senate stairs at once,

Senate Staircase carvings have been erroneously labeled as depicting evolution. Like carvings in European Gothic cathedrals, the ornamentation features animals.

demolishing extensive portions of granite, floor arches, and brickwork that Fuller had designed in order to construct the foundation. On June 19, 1883, James Sinclair & Company of New York City signed a contract for $239,354 to build the staircase. The firm was recognized for its masonry construction and stone carving, having captured such prestigious commissions across the nation such as Biltmore, the Vanderbilt mansion in Asheville, North Carolina; the stock exchange building and Bowery Savings Bank in New York; and estates in Newport, Rhode Island. In the 1870s the firm, then known as Sinclair & Milne, had built the Assembly Chamber, Assembly Staircase, and an addition to the Tweed Courthouse in New York City, all designed by Leopold Eidlitz.

Perry got on splendidly with the Capitol architects, Leopold Eidlitz and H. H. Richardson, who continued on annual retainers. At Perry's request, they left their working drawings in his custody. His aim was to carry out their designs faithfully. Still to be completed by Eidlitz were the Senate Staircase and the tower; by Richardson, the Court of Appeals courtroom, the Western Staircase, and the Great Gable of the west facade. The design for the Eastern Approach had to be resolved, but funds had not yet been made available. As it turned out, this exterior stairway was Isaac Perry's one distinctly personal contribution to the design of the Capitol.

The Senate Staircase carried still further the penchant of Eidlitz for mingling the Moorish-Saracenic note with Victorian Gothic. With the warm cooperation of Perry—who had a keen taste for stone carving—the architect embroidered the four-story stairway with delicate arabesques. An intricate series of graceful half arches climbs the stairway, and they are bordered all the way by arabesques in a series of rectangular frames. No two figures are duplicated.

Other distinctions went into the stairway, which architectural critics praised as one of the most original and vigorous works of the Gothic Revival. Long famous—though by no means a unique device—is the nine-foot wheel, or rose window, in the balustrade between the third and fourth levels.

The *New York Times* later proclaimed that "There is a wonderful wealth of carved work in this staircase, all of it thoroughly thought out in design. The motives are zoological as well as floral. In each of the pier capitals is a grotesque beast. The

Senate Staircase, rising to the fifth floor

rosettes of the bases are filled with comic monsters conforming to their outlines. At the top of a buttress stands a colossal heraldic beast, modeled and carved with great spirit. . . . All this decoration is done from drawings. But a clever modeler furnishes in addition, for the points of the cusps, bosses of heads which recall the grotesqueness of the Middle Ages in everything but the frequent improprieties of the ancient examples."[6]

Perry improved upon Eidlitz's original design by increasing the natural light in the Senate and Assembly staircases. Perry described his solution in his 1883 annual report to the Senate:

Gothic rose wheel in the Senate Staircase

Thirty-one openings have been cut through the immensely thick walls dividing the staircases from the corridors, for the admission of light. Seven of them are through the walls of the old staircase, which are now being dressed with Dorchester freestone of elaborate design, corresponding with the surrounding work. The openings which have been cut through the walls of the southeastern staircase are being dressed with reddish colored freestone, same as used in the construction of the staircase. Openings have also been made through the walls that cross the corridors from north to south and other openings, deemed too small, have been enlarged. In this way the light of the corridors and rooms have been greatly increased and the appearance of the corridors much improved.[7]

The red freestone, which was particularly adaptable to fine carving, was imported from Scotland—Corsehill sandstone. Its advantage was that when first quarried, it was rather soft, but it hardened slowly on exposure to the air, and when rubbed down, it felt like polished wood. This stone could actually be hand cut by the carver, rather than hammered. It worked out so well on the Senate Staircase that it became the principal stone for the Great Western Staircase.

The Senate Staircase was completed in 1885, while the Great Western was just being started.[8] Grover Cleveland by then had gone on to the White House. One of the high moments of Isaac Perry's career was when President Cleveland, on an official visit to Albany, called for him and asked to be shown the status of work on the Capitol, especially the finished stairway. At the end of the tour, the president said, "Perry, come down to Washington, and I will show you some fine buildings, but none like this."[9]

Simultaneously with the start on the western stairway, Isaac Perry began pressing the new State Library forward. The Great Western Staircase was to be the approach to the library's main entrance. Ever since its birth, the library had been something of an orphan in State government, and Perry seems to have been anxious to make amends. Mounting library acquisitions had overflowed the annex behind the Capitol, and the ever-present menace of fire was whispered from time to time. The library's

Griffin on the Senate Staircase

hopes soared with word that the new Capitol would provide the generous space of the third and fourth floors across the entire eastern front of the structure, a length of 300 feet, a width of 47 feet, with a glorious view across the Hudson Valley from its windows. Meanwhile, the Senate occupied the small but exquisite chamber that Leopold Eidlitz had designed for the Court of Appeals on the second floor. The development of the library's new home could not be expected until the Senate Chamber was finished. The Senate moved in toward the end of its 1881 session.

The State Library project received its first shock when Governor Alonzo B. Cornell disclosed that the august justices had rejected Eidlitz's Court of Appeals chamber and coveted instead the third floor space assigned to the library. As Richardson went to work on that courtroom, the library staff was mollified by the promise of commensurate space and elegance across the western rear of the Capitol, even though this meant a major redrafting of architectural plans. It soon became obvious that Isaac Perry meant to carry out Governor Grover Cleveland's mandate to the letter—to erect a substantial yet economical building.

The second jolt came for the library on July 13, 1883, when Perry notified the Board of Regents that "In order to progress with the work on the New Capitol building to advantage and with economy, it has become necessary to remove the State Library building, which I have determined to do. Rooms in

the New Capitol building, which I will cause to be fitted up in a suitable manner, have been assigned."[10] The demolition was to be completed by October 1. In effect, this was a ten-week eviction notice.

To what rooms in the Capitol? The answer was the vacated Court of Appeals courtroom and the Golden Corridor running alongside it—a showpiece which continued to attract a stream of sightseers. In all good faith, Perry solemnly assured the Regents and the state librarian, Dr. Henry Homes, that the awkward expedient was but "temporary" and that the permanent quarters would surely be ready by the summer of 1884. Needless to say, the courtroom and the splendiferous corridor could not begin to contain the entire holdings of the library (126,000 volumes). Books, documents, manuscript collections, and bound newspapers had to be stashed in adjacent office spaces, even in the dungeon-like Capitol basement, subject to damage. The librarians acclimated themselves to making the best of a bad situation for less than a year, in the expectation that a virtual paradise would be their reward. Both they and Perry were in for a rude awakening.

The fickle winds of politics soon stymied Perry's best intentions. After two years in Albany, Grover Cleveland had moved on to Washington. A radically reduced appropriation compelled

State Library main reading room, ca. 1895

Perry to lay off 725 workmen. Year dragged after year as the library suffered through its cramped ordeal. In 1888 a *New York Times* correspondent summed up its sorry plight, saying the library had been "cribbed, coffined, and confined in quarters never intended and entirely unsuited for it." Pointing out that New York could boast the finest state library in the Union, he went on: "The manner in which this treasure is sheltered is a curiosity in the treatment of great libraries, a disgrace to the State, and a triumph in the art of cheese-paring practiced spasmodically by the Legislature."[11]

To top off its troubles, the library learned of its real physical danger—in common with that of the Assembly on the floor above—as fissures began to appear and stone fragments fell from the fabulous groined-arch canopy. The ceiling and supports of the Golden Corridor were showing ominous cracks as well.

Finally, a strongly worded protest from the Board of Regents to the Legislature brought action in the form of a specific appropriation ($147,260) to finish up the library rooms. Before the end of 1889, the State Library, with a surge of relief, bade adieu to the Golden Corridor and moved upstairs into an environment acclaimed as the handsomest of any library in the nation. There it became the near neighbor of both the Senate and Assembly chambers. Isaac Perry had done himself proud with the first major compartment on which he was able to make his own individual impress.

The prodigal space had been broken up into twenty rooms, of which eleven were reading rooms. Woodwork was of quartered oak, and the balusters and newels of connecting stairways were expertly carved. The central feature was the main reading room, rising loftily through two generous stories to an apex of 56 feet. The sumptuous hall was 73 feet long, 42 feet wide, and comparable in size with the Senate Chamber. It had double tiers of galleries along both sides, and stone archways of Romanesque style, supported by colonnades at either end. The pillars of the colonnades were of polished red granite. The massive arches had richly carved beads at the soffits and carved corbels. On the east wall were two Medina sandstone chimneypieces with carved lintels and shelves. Perry pronounced the room as being of a "highly impressive character on account of its size and architectural treatment."[12]

The law library consisted of five rooms with 12,500 linear feet of quartered-oak shelving. A distinctive Knoxville marble chimneypiece adorned the space adjacent to the main reading room. The general library was composed of six reading rooms, a cloakroom, and two toilet rooms.

Meanwhile, Perry had been finishing up the west facade—the most sophisticated face the Capitol has to show to the world. The main feature of this wall is the Great Gable, which, because of its elaborate ornamentation, required a vast amount of skilled labor. Nothing on the exterior of the building so richly repays

Great Gable on the west facade

Great Western Staircase, upper section

scrutiny as this gable, measuring over 82 feet at its base and nearly 66 feet high. It is lavishly carved—even to a pair of winged Babylonian lions—and its tympanum is patterned with raised circles separated by bars. The design for the massive finial at its peak was done by Alexander Wadsworth Longfellow, a nephew of the poet and at that time a draftsman for Richardson.

The New York Capitol was one of the first public buildings in the United States to be electrically lighted. The year before Perry's arrival, the lighting installation had begun, and "dynamo machines" were put in the basement for the power plant. The commission reported adoption of the Maxim incandescent light, "a steady, clear white light, perfectly natural and easy for the eye, which burns in a hermetically sealed exhausted glass bulb, entirely without combustion, and therefore does not consume

the oxygen, or heat or in any manner vitiate the atmosphere."[13] Weston arc lights flickered in the main corridors. Perry finished the electrification of the Capitol and reported in 1885 that 940 incandescent lamps were operating, some of them in the legislative chambers.

Perry's troubles had begun within a year of his appointment when the Legislature made a drastic cut in appropriation and had laid off more than seven hundred men. At that stage, he was naive enough to believe that a personal appeal to the Senate and Assembly would help. Rather plaintively, he said, "I do not wish to be understood as intending or assuming to dictate to the Legislature what appropriations it should make," but, he went on, "to discharge the present well organized, excellent and faithful force of granite workers and other mechanics, compelling them

Drawing by H. H. Richardson for the
Great Western Staircase

Great Western Staircase

to seek employment elsewhere, would not only subject the State to an incalculable loss, and the large number of workmen to great suffering, but would be contrary to true economy."[14]

Perry had gone to great pains to build up a competent, and what he hoped would be a stable, working corps. He could not hold it together if there were periodic interruptions of work. Repeated layoffs, for lack of funds, were exactly what he began to encounter. Any prospect for finishing the building in three years went glimmering.

Nevertheless, Perry stayed, in defiance of some legislative attempts to get rid of him. In passing an 1886 appropriation bill for the Capitol, the Legislature attached a rider to abolish the position of Commissioner of the Capitol and revert to a board. Governor David B. Hill vetoed the bill for that reason and leaped angrily to Perry's defense: "He is removed without any charges having been presented against him, in the absence of any investigation or hearing, and in the face of the conceded *fact* that he is an honest man and a faithful and competent architect and builder."[15]

The bill was not passed over the veto. The Legislature adopted another tactic—that of withholding appropriations. For two successive years there was no Capitol appropriation at all. Work on the Great Western Staircase came to a complete standstill. The next stratagem was to try to restrict Perry's independence by restoring the Commission system over him. Little by little, the Legislature succeeded in this. But the office of Commissioner of the Capitol remained, and he continued to fill it to the end.

Beloved by the men who worked for him, Perry was familiarly known as "the grand old man of the Capitol." He seemed immune to age. His home was on Hawk Street, only a block from his work. The Capitol was his life, and he was to be seen prowling the building at night and on holidays.

The Great Western Staircase was not far along when its designer, H. H. Richardson, died. He had planned some ornamental carving, but not to the extent to which Perry carried it. Richardson's sketches incorporate carving in bands to highlight significant features such as the arches, window surrounds, and capitals. His drawings show that he had intended some life-sized lions on pedestals at the bottom and female statuary upholding lights near the top.

East and north facades of the Capitol, c. 1890, before the Eastern Approach was constructed

While Perry followed Richardson's plan, he also enriched the planar stone surfaces. Perry described the design process in his annual report as follows: "Many score of drawings and models for capitals, corbels, string courses, etc., have been prepared and a large number of works executed from them. The ornamentation of each distinct ornament is different, yet Romanesque in its character . . . there is no other work where the artisans have given more artistic and liberal treatment to the work."[16] It has been said that Perry made the Great Western Staircase a stone carvers' paradise.

The Great Western Staircase is nicknamed the Million Dollar Staircase. It more than deserves the label. The actual cost was in the neighborhood of $1.5 million. The stairwell measures 77 by 70 feet and in height is 119 feet to the skylight. Two steam engines in the attic powered the derricks. The one above the staircase was used to set the stones in place, while the outside crane hoisted materials needed for the interior work. The second

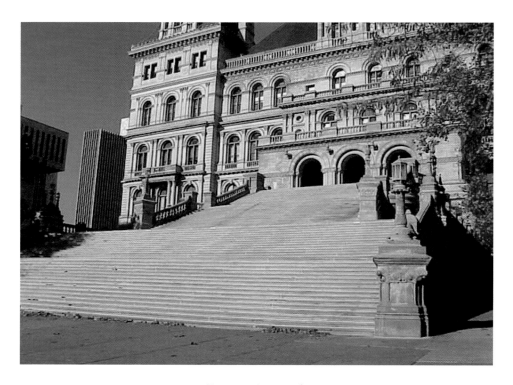

Eastern Approach

steam engine drove the planer, circular saws, lathes, and other machinery for cabinetry work. Perry described the plan thus:

> The stairs, starting from the grand lobby on the west side and the corridor on the east side, meet at a central landing ten feet square, having risen about one-third of the height of the story. From this landing, they branch to the north and south, and after rising another third of the height of the story, each run stops at broad landings at the north and south walls. From each of these landings the stairs start again both east and west and accomplish the remainder of the distance to the next floor.
>
> All the runs and the landings will be supported by arches and groined vaults of stone. The arches carrying the stairs are ramped ellipses and accommodate themselves to the slope of the stairs in a very graceful manner. . . . The vaults . . . are remarkably intricate, requiring absolute geometrical accuracy in their construction.[17]

Periodic layoffs and lack of funds doubled the construction timeline. It was begun in 1884. Ten years later, Perry said in a report that the actual working time had been five and one-half years. While it was structurally completed in 1897, carving went on a year longer. Before it was entirely finished, two governors, Levi P. Morton and Frank S. Black, had walked up the Great Western Staircase on their way to inauguration.

Then, at long last, money was made available for the Eastern Approach. The "advanced terrace" idea of Eidlitz and Richardson, never more than a tentative proposal, was discarded in favor of a stairway, but a more pretentious one than Thomas Fuller had envisioned.

Here was Isaac Perry's supreme chance to prove his worth as an architect in his own right. The front staircase—thanks to the workings of time, fate, and the Legislature—was purely Isaac Perry's creation. He designed it in the Romanesque style and yet was not imitative of his predecessors. Not unexpectedly, he turned the stone carvers loose upon it.

Wise, now, in the ways of politicians, Perry deliberately laid the foundations for the entire staircase all at once, and he got granite on top of them as fast as possible. He was not taking any chances of having somebody curtail the dimensions.[18] The stairway was begun in 1891 and was virtually the last thing done on the outside of the building. It extends out from the front of the building a distance of 166 feet, 7 inches. Cuyler Reynolds, writing in the *Architectural Record* in 1899, described the Eastern Approach as

> a graceful flight of steps 175 feet from the building. The long stretches of balustrade from landing to landing are each made in one piece of granite. At all advantageous points carving of the finest kind is to be met. Having ascended 77 steps, one stands upon a broad plateau before the entrance. . . . There is hardly any space on the main approach that is not carved. The American eagle and turkey of life-size are ornaments on the face of two large granite blocks in this approach, and heads of a buffalo and of a lion, the size of nature, give dignity to the terminals of the driveway under the front flight of steps. Some of the stones weigh 26 tons.[19]

The odd thing about this front staircase is that relatively few people make use of it. Its seventy-seven steps are impractical for the daily business of the Capitol, and many legislators can truthfully say they never have climbed them.

The final treatment of the east facade presented a problem. Perry proposed to give it a gable in the center, similar to the Great Gable of the west facade. There was to be a 16-foot projection of the front to support it. Doubt as to the capacity of the foundations to hold the weight compelled the abandonment of the gable. Reluctantly, Perry compromised the facade with a recessed balcony over the entrance portico. Instead of the gable, he placed a trio of dormers at the roof's edge.

Perry, the "grand old man of the Capitol," was still actively at work at the age of seventy-five, a straight and sturdy figure. Toward the last, his duties were curtailed when Governor Black placed the superintendent of public works, George Aldridge, in charge of finishing the Capitol. In his January 1898 Annual Message, Governor Black directed that the building would be completed, the grounds laid out and work sheds removed before October.

One year later, Theodore Roosevelt became governor, on January 1, 1899. On February 4, Roosevelt removed Isaac Perry from the office of Capitol Commissioner.

Perry returned to his old home in Binghamton to live with his memories.

In all its checkered history, no one man had labored so devotedly for so long a term to get the New York Capitol built as Isaac Perry.

SCIENTIFIC AMERICAN

[Entered at the Post Office of New York, N. Y., as Second Class Matter. Copyrighted, 1888, by Munn & Co.]

WEEKLY JOURNAL OF PRACTICAL INFORMATION, ART, SCIENCE, MECHANICS, CHEMISTRY, AND MANUFACTURES

Vol. LVIII.—No. 10.
[NEW SERIES.]

NEW YORK, MARCH 10, 1888.

[$3.00 per Year.

Assembly Chamber, with trestle supporting the cracked ceiling, *Scientific American*, March 1888

CHAPTER TEN

THE CASE OF THE UNFORTUNATE CEILING

Danforth E. Ainsworth

MISFORTUNE PLAGUED THE WONDERFUL ASSEMBLY CEILING OF LEOPOLD EIDLITZ.
After the first cracked stone was replaced, four new cracks appeared.
The 1882 Legislature authorized a commission of two architects and a civil
engineer—Professor W. P. Trowbridge, an engineer from Columbia University; Professor Charles Babcock, an architect from Cornell University;
and George B. Post, a noted practicing architect—to make an independent
study of the chamber's "safety and durability." These experts decided that
the foundations under the four main columns of the chamber were loaded to
the extreme limit of safety, that unequal settlement had occurred, that "the
continued stability of the vaulted ceiling is a matter of doubt," and that it
had been "an error of judgment to erect that most delicate of all architectural
devices, a stone groined ceiling, and particularly one of unusual span and
weight, on foundations not absolutely secured against uneven settlement."
They recommended "with great reluctance" that the architect be instructed
to remove all the stone vaulting and substitute a wooden ceiling.[1]

Governor Alonzo B. Cornell called a conference and showed the report.
It was taken for granted that the Assembly would refuse to occupy its
chamber at the next session. In anticipation, the desks and chairs of members were removed to the Court of Appeals chamber on the floor below,
just then being vacated for the newer courtroom.

The architect rushed to the defense of his work. Eidlitz, Richardson & Company, in a communication to the governor, took issue with the adverse report, blaming the fractures on the normal settling of a heavy building. The partners asked for and were granted permission to make repairs at their own expense. The Assembly took them at their word that the ceiling was then "a perfectly sound and permanent structure." The desks and chairs were moved back.

The deterioration of the sandstone continued. More than once during the 1880s Eidlitz had urged the Trustees of Public

Assembly Chamber, ca. 1880

Buildings to make further repairs. In May 1887 he wrote Assemblyman James W. Husted, chairman of the Trustees, asking that a new board of experts be appointed to examine the ceiling. "Our professional reputation," Eidlitz stated, "should not be permitted to be assailed, nor should we be held responsible for the integrity of the work while our recommendations to do necessary work for its completion and make necessary repairs for its maintenance are not acted upon."[2]

In October a seven-pound chunk of stone was found one morning calmly reposing on the lush red carpet of the Assembly Chamber.

The fall of the stone did not become public knowledge until the Legislature met in January 1888. Then the repercussions jolted the Capitol, figuratively, to its very foundations. Legislation languished for weeks, as the 128 members of the Assembly were distracted by the tons of masonry above their heads.

"In my opinion," declaimed Thomas C. Clark, an engineer, "no Assemblyman can sit in this chamber without the thought of an awful doom, perhaps, before him."[3] The general public was apprised of the stability of the ceiling during January and February 1888 as newspaper headlines announced the ceiling was "Falling Down in Chunks" and "Its Condition is Unsafe."

A resolution was introduced to direct the state superintendent of insurance to take out a $25,000 insurance policy on the life of each Assemblyman for the duration of the session, the premiums to be paid by the State.

The danger was real and imminent. Stone dust sifted down upon desktops. A member found a stone fragment in his seat. John I. Platt of Poughkeepsie collected the chips that fell until he had a dozen—one "as big as a soup-plate"—in a box under his desk, and then displayed them to his colleagues. A Brooklyn Assemblyman soon was exhibiting an even larger stone but was strongly suspected of having brought it back from a weekend at home.

After receiving the warning letter from Leopold Eidlitz the previous May, Governor Hill had considered calling a special session of the Legislature but decided against it because he feared the publicity would excite a "panic" among Assemblymen. Now, with the Assembly back in the Chamber and the spalls tumbling, Eidlitz fired off a really urgent letter to Albany on January 9, 1888. Since his prior appeals had gone unheeded, he said, "we cannot, in reason, be held responsible for possible accidents." And he went on, "But, inasmuch as, by reason of the long neglect above referred to, such accidents are possible, we deem it our duty to respectfully protest against the further occupancy of the north wing of the Capitol in its present condition; and we request that you will direct that the Assembly Chamber, the State Library and the offices in that part of the building, be closed until definite action, in accordance with our repeated recommendation, shall have been taken."[4]

With the architect himself hinting darkly of "accidents," the governor could no longer keep the Legislature uninformed. He summoned committee chairmen of both Houses and laid before them the two Eidlitz letters, remarking that, if he were an Assemblyman, he would not occupy the room a single day. Assemblyman Ainsworth, chairman of the Appropriations Committee, told the Assembly about the letters.

The Assembly already had a bill in the works for a special commission to study the ceiling once again. Its members would be State Engineer John Bogart; Thomas C. Clarke, the engineer who designed the Poughkeepsie railroad bridge; and Richard M. Upjohn, the prominent New York architect who instigated the attack by the American Institute of Architects on the Advisory Board in 1876. The Senate returned the bill with an amendment requiring this commission to submit, with its report, an estimate of the cost of removing the ceiling. This ruffled feathers in the Assembly. An angry debate ensued, in which the Senate was charged with quibbling about a "life-and-death matter," but the bill passed.

The three experts went to work immediately. Entering the loft above the ceiling, they discovered a fresh crack at the apex of the main vault. It was big enough so they could look down and see the floor of the chamber, 56 feet below.

Although the commission had been given forty days in which to prepare its report, it rushed an interim report to the Assembly saying that "The whole ceiling is in a dangerous condition, more or less cracked, and showing signs of unexpected pressure. As the ribs were originally none too large to resist the pressure, in their present condition they are still less able to do their work. A time must come, and we believe very soon, when

without warning, one or more of these overtaxed ribs must give way. When that happens the whole ceiling will fall. We recommend that the Assembly Chamber and the story behind it be immediately vacated; that strong and properly supportive centres be put up at once [and] that the whole ceiling be taken down as soon as possible."[5] The emergency report was read just before a Friday adjournment in early February. A stunned silence ensued.

Upon reconvening Monday night, the legislators had dropped their pose of bravado. Fully half the Assembly seats were vacant. Those members present were looking not so much at the Speaker as at the ceiling. The session lasted exactly twelve minutes. A headline said: "Lawmakers Demoralized."

Next morning many Assemblymen appeared with overcoats on and hats in hand, and remained standing. A report was heard that the only other suitable room was the Senate Chamber; and that the Senate—with its much smaller membership—might easily occupy the Assembly Parlor for the time being. A resolution was sent across to the Senate asking if that body would lend the use of its chamber to the Assembly.

The Senate debated the request very briefly and refused.

Finally, amid mutterings about the "selfish Senate," a decision was made to try the Assembly Parlor—a very fine room, but designed only for lounging and committee sessions. The desks were jammed in cheek by jowl. A board platform was erected for the Speaker. The worst drawback of all was lack of ventilation. Frequent recesses had to be taken to air out the room.

Meanwhile, Isaac Perry had worked out a scheme for shoring up the ceiling and making the chamber habitable for the remainder of the session. Both houses adjourned for a week and went home while the change was being made. Isaac Perry believed that temporary supports could be used to stabilize the ceiling until the building had finished settling. The bracing was completed by late February and described in the Albany *Evening Journal*: "The centre twin uprights which rise on either side of the stenographer and in the places occupied by the desks of Mssrs. Weed of Clinton, Smith of Sullivan, McKenna of New York and Acker of Steuben are braced with cross beams diagonally from 19 feet above the floor to the staging and resemble the leg of a grain elevator, or an inverted span of a bridge. These uprights are 30 inches through and 16 feet apart. . . . The staging is 42 feet from the floor and supported by straight trusses which extend from the centre upright supports of Georgia pine to others placed against the wall. Each length is made doubly secure with heavy rods stretched over bridges of iron. The staging extends under the small vaulted ceilings as well, and is considered of sufficient strength to stop any spawl that might fall."[6]

Unsightly as these makeshift surroundings were, the Assembly found one decided improvement: the acoustics were very much better!

Leopold Eidlitz, in New York, was deeply distressed and spoke his thoughts in letters to his firm's surviving partner, Frederick Law Olmsted. He was hopeful that the Bogart commission would recommend the rebuilding of the ceiling, not its utter removal. "Both Bogart and Clarke tell me that it is their

Assembly Chamber, ca. 1890, showing the new coffered ceiling

intention to do so," Eidlitz wrote, "and that so far they see no technical reason why it should not be done." He continued, "Our status in Albany and my reputation as an architect measurably depend upon this, and a little friendly influence will do much good at this time. If I am right in thinking that you can personally do much good with Mr. Bogart, I wish you would come on to see him on purpose."[7]

But the battle Eidlitz put up to save his temperamental ceiling was doomed to failure. The Bogart commission's final report, dated April 26, 1888, recommended total elimination of the stone groined-vault ceiling and its replacement by one of wood or metal. In view of the improved acoustics noted with the temporary plank staging, it was suggested that the new ceiling should be flat.

Serious cracks, meanwhile, had been found in the Assembly Staircase and in the Golden Corridor, as well. The commission recommended extensive repairs for both of these Eidlitz show-pieces. The Golden Corridor could not be saved. Within two years it was demolished, and its space partitioned off into committee rooms. (Today the area of the once-celebrated corridor is occupied by various offices of the Executive Department.)

The Legislature passed a bill appropriating $278,922 in late April 1888—with certain strings attached. It specified that the work of removing the old ceiling in the Assembly Chamber and constructing a new one was to be in the complete charge of the superintendent of public buildings, Charles B. Andrews—bypassing the Capitol commissioner, Isaac Perry. Moreover, it established an Assembly Ceiling Committee, which was empowered to employ a special architect for the job and to award the contract ($40,000 of the appropriation was earmarked for repair of the staircase).

Governor David B. Hill wanted very much to veto the bill. He could see no reason why the work should not be under the control of Isaac Perry, and he was suspicious that the Ceiling Committee would be an entering wedge toward putting Perry back under the thumb of a commission. "Such a committee," he said in his accompanying message, "not infrequently constitutes the worst kind of a commission, and oftentimes leads to deals, jobs, abuses and corruption. . . . An emergency is presented. If I refuse to approve this bill, the Assembly ceiling must remain in

its present disgraceful, if not dangerous, condition, for another year and during another session. The bill is only permitted to become a law because of the extraordinary existing situation."[8] Governor Hill must be credited with remarkable foresight. The legislative stage was now set for the unhappy sequel.

Charles Andrews had few discernible qualifications for being superintendent of public buildings. An investigator later referred to him as "a superintendent who frankly acknowledges his own incompetence."[9] The Ceiling Committee allowed him $3,500, on top of his regular salary, for supervising the ceiling job. And it left it to him to get bids on the contract.

Andrews brought in six bids for the committee's action. The lowest was $270,150, submitted by an Albany building contractor, John Snaith, later revealed as a close personal friend of Andrews. Only in retrospect did it occur to anyone how close the bid was to the actual appropriation, with enough margin to cover Andrews's extra pay and the fee of a special architect.

It was Andrews who recommended an architect to the Ceiling Committee—one Arthur H. Rowe, who maintained that he was a professor of architecture at Cornell University. Rowe had been on the Cornell faculty for a short time but was dismissed when the university discovered that he had obtained the post with false credentials. It was revealed that Rowe had been one of the workmen brought over from England by Ezra Cornell to erect his Llenroc mansion and that Rowe had become an intimate of John Snaith while they were in Ithaca. According to the *New York Times,* Rowe could not "design a chicken coop" and Andrews was "an unscrupulous person utterly lacking in a sense of official propriety." At any rate, the committee engaged Rowe, and he it was who drew the plans for the new ceiling—and later altered them, at Andrews's behest.

After awarding the contract to John Snaith, the Assembly Ceiling Committee adjourned and went home. Not one of its five members came near Albany all that summer of 1888 to see how the work was progressing.

Snaith subcontracted the Assembly Staircase repair job to Timothy J. Sullivan, another Albany contractor, who likewise turned out to be a bosom friend of Andrews. (Before it was all over, this trio of Snaith, Sullivan, and Andrews would be depicted as "a closed corporation.")

The magnificent ceiling had lasted precisely ten years. Now the stone was stripped from its gracefully arched vaults and carted off to find its way into various Albany buildings—many of them other Snaith contracts. In its place, but 14 feet lower, a flat wooden ceiling was carpentered in—quite similar in appearance to the Senate ceiling. It sealed off the renowned Hunt murals. While this new ceiling was ornamental enough, with its carved-oak beams and deep-sunk coffers, it was architecturally incongruous. It truncated the tops of arches and was too low over the tiers of stained-glass windows. The ponderous granite pillars were never intended to uphold so light a structure.

Assembly Chamber, drawing of spandrels just below the ceiling, inscribed with the words "Papier Mache or oak"

When the 1889 Assembly convened in the remodeled Chamber, the members at least did not have to fret about anything falling on their heads, and they were overjoyed to find how much more clearly they could hear one another speak. But another kind of trouble was brewing. Its nature was hinted in a newspaper dispatch: "It seems that the fine rich oaken ceiling of the reconstructed Assembly Chamber is not even paper, as was recently supposed, but mere plaster; and it isn't even good plaster, but flakes and crumbles when subjected to the tension of heat and cold."[10]

A rumor had spread that plaster of paris—not carved oak—had gone into the ceiling. Assemblyman George S. Batcheller had taken a trip to Albany while the work was in progress and spirited away a strip of ornamental beading. Triumphantly he now pulled it forth and passed it around to his associates, declaring, "It is not made of papier-mâché, but of plaster of paris!"[11] Legislators and taxpayers alike were by this time so hypersensitive to the Assembly ceiling that they were ready to believe anything said of it. The Committee on Appropriations was to conduct hearings. On January 24, a panel of experts was selected to examine the new ceiling—Charles B. Brush, University of New York civil engineering professor; Archimedes Russell, Syracuse architect; Albert H. Chester, Hamilton College chemistry professor; and Stanford White, New York architect. Loose statements got into print to the effect that the alleged plaster of paris was starting to crumble and that soon the entire ceiling would disintegrate.

By February 16 the experts presented their findings and concluded that the drawings prepared by Rowe were vague and incomplete. They stated that the contract had been violated because material changes had been substituted: the ironwork differed from the specifications; the plans called for 768 panels in the coffered ceiling, but only 396 panels were constructed. Eight pilasters of cut stone were to be lengthened and capped to correspond to granite columns, but uncapped extensions were made instead. The woodwork was not entirely of quartered oak; it was not the first-rate cabinet work specified, nor had it received the specified finish. The panels were to be either of flat oak or vaulted papier-mâché. Papier-mâché was to be used only in the ceiling panels.[12]

The furor over plaster of paris disappeared with news that it had not been used, that nothing was beginning to flake, and that the Saratoga legislator was wrong in saying there was no carved oak in the ceiling. The frames of the panels were of carved oak, but the sunken coffers were of molded papier-mâché, painted to resemble oak. When the inquiry disclosed this fact, the public got the impression that papier-mâché was a flimsy product that would rapidly fall apart. In reality, it was a quite durable and reputable material that was widely used at the time in architectural ornamentation. It was not cheap compared to wood. The ceiling of the Metropolitan Opera House in New York was cited as one example of the appropriate use of papier-mâché.

Superintendent Andrews readily admitted that the coffers were of papier-mâché, stating that the specifications had allowed the contractor to choose between it and quartered oak. He and the contractor had chosen papier-mâché because it would better withstand the heat of the room rising to the ceiling, maintaining that the oak coffers would soon have cracked at the typical 70 degree temperature. Snaith claimed the Assembly ceiling was the best of any in the Capitol.

As a matter of fact, the papier-mâché panels survived very well. When the Capitol fire raged through the west side of the building in 1911, the papier-mâché panels saved the Assembly Chamber from being fully engulfed in flames. The ceiling panels remained until the mid-1930s without noticeable deterioration and were then replaced with plain, uncarved wood.

The issue was not so much the fact of the papier-mâché as it was whether or not the specifications had permitted the alternative. This question never was settled satisfactorily. The written specifications produced at the inquiry said that "The panels are to be quartered oak, as shown, properly glued up and finished, or of papier mâché, as may be directed by the superintendent." Only one of the five members of the Ceiling Committee testified that he could remember seeing the words "papier-mâché" in the specifications at the award of the contract. When all was said, a dual question was left dangling: either the other four members of the committee had not bothered to read the specifications, or someone had tampered with the specifications after the contract was awarded.

The Appropriations Committee reported on February 25. It found the Assembly Ceiling Committee to have been guilty of "gross carelessness" but laid the principal blame at the door of the Legislature itself for having entrusted the direction of the job to "a confessedly incompetent man, and inexperienced committee . . . to the exclusion of the competent state officer," Isaac Perry. The report conceded that the contract did permit the alternative between oak and papier-mâché. The report also charged that the architect, Arthur Rowe, had made changes in the plans during the course of the work, under Charles Andrews's instructions, and that the changes were always in the direction of greater profits for the contractors. It criticized Andrews for "negligence in not properly supervising the work and insisting upon strict compliance with the contract." It recommended that the Ceiling Committee refuse to accept the ceiling as it stood, that Andrews's duties be transferred to Perry, who should then compel the contractor to make good on his shortcuts.[13]

The board of experts (whose architect members were Stanford White and Archimedes Russell) had reported that the papier-mâché was "eminently suited for the vaulted panels" but that the contractor had been remiss in other respects, such as using that material for the spandrels and beading. The dynamite in their report was the estimate they made of the actual value of the work accomplished—$165,000, allowing for a fair profit. This meant that Snaith and company had made a profit of $106,000.

Some Assemblymen felt that the report of the Appropriations Committee was too weak, especially in its slap on the wrist for Andrews. The Legislature already had sent a resolution to the Trustees of Public Buildings urging the suspension of Andrews on grounds of dereliction of duty, but the trustees held off acting upon it. Determined not to let the matter drop, the Assembly named a special committee to carry on a second, more thorough, inquiry, one object of which was to ascertain into what "channels" Snaith's alleged $106,000 profit had flowed. The chairman of this committee was Assemblyman Hamilton Fish Jr., of Putnam County.

When the Fish committee opened its hearings on March 4, it found itself embarrassingly short of key witnesses. Snaith and Rowe were absent from the city. Snaith's bookkeeper was reported as being in Bermuda "for his health." A local jeweler wanted for questioning also had taken a sudden trip to Bermuda (it was said that he had sold an expensive piece of jewelry to Snaith as a gift for Mrs. Andrews). Mrs. Andrews, when sought, was reported to be visiting relatives in Boston; later evidence indicated she was actually hidden in the Albany home of a brother.

John Snaith was located in Philadelphia, where he had fled with a gripsack full of ledgers and account books. Arthur Rowe turned up in Memphis, Tennessee, after visiting Snaith in Philadelphia. Neither could be extradited, the inquiry not being a court of law, and they would not return voluntarily.

The Fish committee took what testimony it could and reported in May, concluding that "Andrews, Sullivan and Snaith combined to defraud the people of the State" and that the profit on the contract had been nearer to $120,000. It recommended the removal of Andrews from his state office; called the attention of the district attorney to the evidence it had taken, suggesting that he lay it before a grand jury; and prodded the attorney general to start action against the three men to recover money "of which they have despoiled the state."[14]

The Assembly had craved a stronger report and now had it. Inexplicably, the legislators voted to reject it and to accept instead the prior report of the Appropriations Committee. This

Hamilton Fish Jr.

vacillating behavior prompted a newspaper headline: "Fish Inquiry in Vain."

A fortnight later John Snaith appeared back in town, driving his phaeton coolly through the streets of Albany.

Not only was Snaith back—he filed a claim against the State for $40,000. This was the amount of the final payment on his contract which the State had withheld when the ceiling scandal erupted.

Andrews was fired as superintendent of public buildings in May 1889 and succeeded by Edwin K. Burnham. Two successive Albany County grand juries failed to bring indictments against the trio.

That autumn, Attorney General Charles F. Tabor started an action in Oneida County against Snaith, Sullivan, and Andrews to recover $250,563 as damages "occasioned by fraud in repairing the State Capitol." The defendants won a change of venue back to Albany County. Before the case got on the calendar, the Appellate Court granted a motion vacating the order for their arrest.

Snaith's claim for $40,000 against the State was finally disallowed by the Board of Claims. His profit, at least, was reduced by that much.

Assembly Chamber, restored gallery

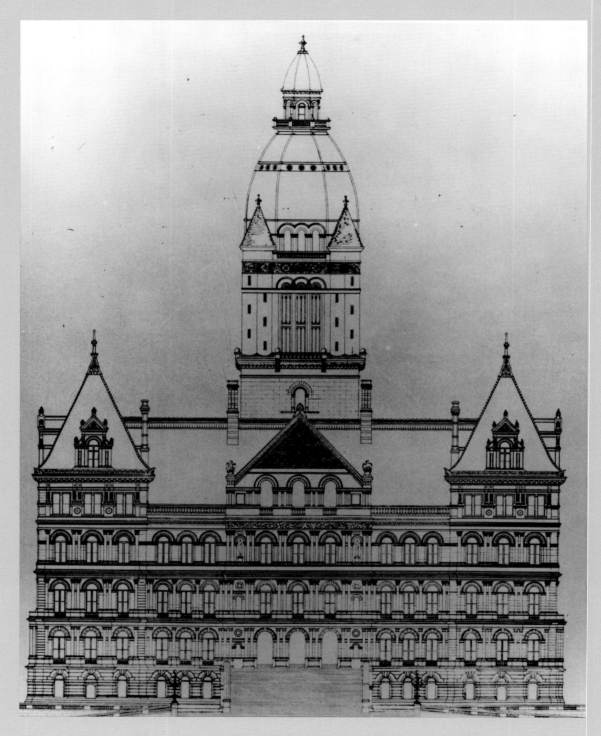

East elevation, with gable inked in, possibly by Isaac Perry

CHAPTER ELEVEN

THE TOWER THAT
NEVER WAS

Proposed Capitol tower, ca. 1890

IT WAS TAKEN FOR GRANTED THAT THE CAPITOL MUST BE CROWNED WITH A dome. A Capitol without a dome would be as preposterous as a church without a steeple. Albany at that time was a city of domes. The city hall had a fine dome, and so did the adjacent state hall. The existing Capitol and the Albany Academy had their graceful cupolas. A downtown hotel was splendidly domed.

Some of the competition drawings for a new Capitol did not include a dome. The Commissioners of the Land Office, who held a veto power, made it plain that they would not approve a design without a dome. Therefore, Thomas Fuller and Arthur Gilman gave them a magnificent design. It would spear the sky at 320 feet, and then there would be a cast-iron eagle or a statue on the apex. It would be the focal point of Albany. Venturesome sightseers would be able to climb spiral stairs to an observation platform where they would get a stunning view. It was so high in the drawings that it always was referred to as a tower rather than a dome.

The grand tower was to be placed toward the front, or east side, of the building. It would make an end wall for the central court. The interior dimensions would be 66 by 66 feet in plan. The solid granite walls at that stage would be nine feet thick. At the second level, visitors could stand in a rotunda, designated in the floor plans as Tower Hall, and look up a clear 75 feet to a concave, frescoed ceiling.

As fast as the outer walls grew, so did the ponderous walls to support the tower. Its footings were sunk seven feet deeper than the rest. The granite blocks of its foundation averaged four tons. The blocks were "stepped out" at the base, giving its walls a pedestal 20 feet wide. There was to be no skimping here!

Then, in the 1870s, came the Advisory Board. While Eidlitz, Richardson, and Olmsted had a good deal to say about the tower, they did not propose to eliminate it. But they doubted that its shape "will long be regarded as entirely felicitous." They drew a new plan making it stubbier and rounder and giving it a German Romanesque flavor. They deplored the fact that the tower was not located above some room or central space "of specially noble character," or at least a more ample rotunda. It was, in effect, "an edifice by itself."[1]

Professor Charles Eliot Norton of Harvard, in his exchange of letters with Olmsted during the "Battle of the Styles," expressed doubts:

> I regret the necessity of the dome. It is unmeaning, has no aesthetic or constructive relation with the main building, but is a mere piece of very costly show. It will be a permanent monument not of culture but of barbarism. . . . I suppose the work had gone so far that you were forced to retain this too conspicuous feature— and, being so, you certainly have given it a very effective form, and one not incongruous with the rest of the building.[2]

Construction of the tower was assigned to Eidlitz when, for practical purposes, he and Richardson divided the building between them.

Many stonecutters worked on it exclusively. By the mid-1890s its thick granite walls stood 20 feet above the roofline. A shed protected the opening from the elements. Nearly $1 million had been spent on it. Until then, nobody had done any audible worrying about its weight.

Isaac Perry submitted a plan for finishing the tower. Archimedes Russell, a member of the Capitol Commission, reported that Perry had revised the earlier tower concept "based upon the theory that no more weight can be added to the foundations on which the tower as constructed to its present altitude rests."[3] Perry had made a fresh study and decided that the weight so far was "equivalent to the full sustaining capacity of the earth on which the area of the lowest base course foundations rest."[4]

His proposed solution was to take off the top 26 feet of granite and substitute for the rest of the tower a structural steel skeleton, covered with sheet copper and cast bronze ornaments. The weight of the metal structure, he estimated, would about equal the weight of the granite removed.

AMERICAN ARCHITECT AND BUILDING NEWS, MARCH 11, 1876.

NEW STATE CAPITOL AT ALBANY.
SECTION THROUGH THE PROPOSED DOME.
HELIOTYPE. JAMES R. OSGOOD & CO., BOSTON.

**Section through the proposed tower
showing spiral stairway to a lookout platform**

Foundations for the tower under construction

The restaurant was converted into the Legislative Correspondents' Room, still in use today.

While the tower may have been abandoned because the ground beneath would not support its weight, one cannot resist the thought that perhaps a more powerful reason was economy. In reporting the elimination of the tower, the Capitol Commission itself left a subtle hint for posterity to ponder: "While all this has been accomplished, it has not been done at the sacrifice or denial of the privilege of yet obtaining the grand metal tower should future generations command the courage to attempt it."[8]

After all, the tremendously heavy granite walls that were constructed for the tower, then left uncrowned, have been standing there all these years without catastrophe.

A quarter of a century passed. After World War I a patriotic spirit generated a desire to honor military veterans. Under Governor Alfred E. Smith a project was conceived to create a flag room beneath the 40 foot high rotunda, within the walls of the

Archimedes Russell, a newly appointed member of the Capitol Commission, found Perry's design solution for the metal tower less than noteworthy, writing that "This method of procedure may be of doubtful expediency, venturesome and experimental in an artistic and aesthetic sense, liable perhaps to severe criticism as a cheap and unsubstantial treatment of the crowning feature."[5]

Hurry and economy were now the watchwords. The commission determined that the best thing to do with the tower was get rid of it altogether. Perry's speculations about the weight provided an excellent excuse.

The commission, in 1896, advertised for bids for removing the temporary roof of the tower, lopping off the protruding part of its walls, putting a permanent roof over the space, and creating floors through the open rotunda of the tower on the third, fourth and fifth levels. The added floor areas afforded "valuable and much desired apartments in each story."[6] The fourth story was made into Senate committee rooms.

The third story was "handsomely fitted up for the telegraph and telephone companies, the press and a commodious café."[7]

East wall of the Central Courtyard,
showing a remnant of the masonry tower

Rendering of a two-story rotunda within the tower space

**Flag room on the first floor, planned as the
base of the two-story rotunda**

A New York artist, William deLeftwich Dodge, was commissioned in October 1920 to paint the murals at a fee of $42,000. He spent five years painting the mural panels in his home studio, aided by his daughter, Sara, but installation was delayed due to a lack of funding for the rotunda space. The murals were finally installed between November 1928 and February 1929 by Dodge and his assistant, Melio Bellisio. There are 25 paintings on canvas and four decorated panels painted directly on plaster, all surrounded by gilded moldings and plaster ornament. The centerpiece was an embossed female figure, holding a shield and sword, her left foot balanced on an orb. Dodge called her the Goddess of Harmony or Spirit of New York; she symbolizes an American Athena, goddess of both war and peace. Governor Franklin D. Roosevelt dedicated the paintings in 1929.

But the floor beneath had not been removed. It never was. The Great Depression struck, and another fine scheme was abandoned. The space was converted into a mail-and-messenger room for the Executive Department. There the Dodge murals remained unknown to the public—an ornate ceiling for a clerical staff to work beneath. The paintings never were viewed in the perspective for which they were designed. In 1997, the room was rehabilitated and the Dodge murals were restored; today the room functions as a reception room for visitors waiting to meet with the governor and his staff. Down in the basement, the tremendous, stepped-out foundation walls of the tower remain intact. The dungeon-like square space enclosed by them is used as to store architectural salvage.

truncated tower. A substantial portion of the second floor would need to be removed to develop this monumental space as a war memorial. This would then become the Flag Room—a repository of the Civil War keepsakes of the New York State Military Museum. The rotunda would have a dome with murals of the wars in which New York State had participated. The estimated cost of this improvement was $350,000.

Ceiling mural of the *Goddess of Harmony* or *Spirit of New York*
by William deLeftwich Dodge in the Governor's Reception Room

William deLeftwich Dodge

Eastern Approach, architectural drawing, 1890

CHAPTER TWELVE

THE STONE CARVERS

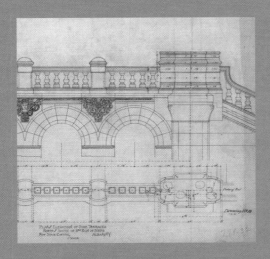

Carving on the Eastern Approach, 1890

A BUILDING WITH SO VORACIOUS AN APPETITE FOR GRANITE DEMANDED AN ARMY of stonecutters. Year after year, these men comprised roughly half of the Capitol's working force. Their numbers exceeded 600 in 1882, when the west walls and pavilions were built up to the roofline. Even during the depression of the 1870s, the carvers earned $5 for a 10 hour day, twice the wage of common laborers. They were drawn largely from quarry communities, many following the granite from New England. A considerable number moved to Albany after working on the U.S. Capitol in Washington.

These were a breed of men unto themselves, proud in their work. They even had their special occupational hazard—the dreaded silicosis that came with breathing too much stone dust. The Capitol being the long-lasting job it was, the stonecutters tended to settle and make homes in Albany, and many raised families in the city and married them off before the building was completed. The surrounding stone sheds were a familiar part of the Capitol scene. This was before the day of pneumatic tools, and the mallet and chisel were the standard instruments of the trade.

A stonecutter had two main responsibilities. The first was to cut a rough stone into a finished block, using a full-scale drawing or a wooden model as a guide. The other task was preparing the surface for the stone carver,

Carving of *Plenty* on the Eastern Approach

chiseling away much of the stone to allow the carver to produce more detailed work such as an ornate capital, incised ornament, or sculptural elements. Unlike a cutter, a stone carver was trained to copy any design into stone, no matter how complex the pattern or how difficult the material was to work.

The stone carvers were an elite corps. Among them were a few who could be ranked as true architectural sculptors and two or three who so sharpened their talent by working on the Capitol that they afterward opened private studios. The Capitol is an amazing repository of the carvers' skill.

The carving done in the 1870s and 1880s was concentrated on the exterior, the Assembly and Senate chambers, the corridors, and the Assembly and Senate staircases. Leopold Eidlitz's designs for the Assembly Chamber and the Senate Staircase enhanced the flat sandstone walls and ceilings with incised ornament. The Assembly Staircase combined pointed-arch arcades, pilasters and columns crowned with robust foliate capitals, and quatrefoil tracery railings with stenciled wall surfaces painted in vermilion, ultramarine, black, and gold. These Gothic Revival designs were translated into stone by master carver James Keefe of Sinclair and Milne of New York City.

Richardson's Senate Chamber achieved its sumptuous quality from the rich use of masonry materials and wood. The stone carving is discrete, confined to roll moldings on the arches, dentil courses, column capitals, and the balusters of the gallery railings. The heavily carved fireplace in Richardson's Court of Appeals courtroom, attributed to John Evans of Boston, was completed under the supervision of Isaac Perry.

Most of the relief carving and the portraiture was created during the 1890s, also under the direction of Isaac Perry during the final phases of construction. The carvers' greatest undertakings were the Great Western Staircase (later dubbed the Million Dollar Staircase) and the Eastern Approach. In general, the sculptured likenesses of the Great Western Staircase are historical, those of the Eastern Approach symbolic.

Not everyone at the time wholeheartedly approved of Perry's passion for carving. Archimedes Russell, an architect and a member of the Capitol Commission in the mid-1890s, criticized the "decorative features" of the Eastern Approach as being "applied indiscriminately and so profusely as to surfeit and disgust the sensibilities."[1] To implement the massive carving campaign, Perry assembled a group of highly skilled designers and carvers. When Perry arrived in Albany in 1883, he was accompanied by his former apprentice, Sanfred O. Lacey. Lacey was initially employed as the foreman of the carvers and recognized in an 1888 newspaper as the "chief designer of most of the superb interior ornamentation of the Capitol."[2] Lacey became Perry's chief draftsman but by 1893 returned to Binghamton to establish his own architectural practice. Louis J. Hinton returned to this country in 1885 after several years in his native England and applied for work on the Capitol as construction of the Great Western Staircase was beginning. Perry engaged him as foreman to supervise the carvers on that staircase. Later, Hinton took on the added duty of designing all the carving. "I was kept busy making free-hand scale drawings," he reminisced in later years, "and laying out the work on the smooth finished surface of the moldings, while still directing the carvers at their work."[3]

Variety was the unyielding rule on that staircase. Not even the smallest of decorative themes could be repeated in different locations. For the sake of authenticity, Hinton hiked about the countryside collecting foliage and flowers for his designs—roses, clematis, trumpet vine, tulips, passionflowers, lilies, and grapevines.

Great Western Staircase, carving of J. Fenimore Cooper,
surrounded by faces of characters in his
Leatherstocking Tales.

Clay model used for carving of J. Fennimore Cooper

Louis Hinton had been born in London, the son of a master carver who had worked on the statue of Horatio Nelson in Trafalgar Square. The boy grew up to be an expert carver. In 1869 he was one of a group of fourteen hand-picked "building trade mechanics" brought from England by Ezra Cornell to build his home in Ithaca, New York. When that job was done, Hinton worked on the terraces and fountains of New York's Central Park, helped Chicago to rebuild after the 1871 fire, and then, partly because of the depressed economic condition of the United States, went back to England.

The position that Hinton found at the Capitol resulted in Albany's becoming his permanent home. While he was foreman of carvers at the Capitol, Hinton had placed his artistically gifted son, Charles, to work among them. The Hintons also worked together on carvings in the Cathedral of All Saints in Albany. Charles Hinton had a career as an artist and sculptor, with a studio in Bronxville.

Perry trusted Louis Hinton implicitly. Hinton's attitude toward Perry was similarly respectful: "It is one of my very pleasant memories to have known and loved him," Hinton wrote. "Mr. Perry paid close attention to the carving. I know

that not a stone was carved nor an idea carried out in model form or otherwise without [his] being in on it from start to finish. He loved the work and passed more time with the men, carving and modeling, than is usual with architects."[4]

Perry's rapt interest in the carvings, and his rigid standards for them, are reflected in the 1895 specifications for completing the upper portions of the Great Western Staircase:

The carving of the corbels, cornices and label moldings is to have deep sinkages and be made free and bold, in accordance with the full-size plaster models.

There must be no feeling of monotony in the design and much variety must be obtained in the decorative work.

Great care is to be taken in carving the heads, as well as the foliage. The whole work is to be cut deep, clean and sharp, so that the light and shadow will be satisfactory to the capitol commissioner.[5]

The Corsehill freestone imported from Scotland, the sandstone used in the Great Western Staircase, gave the carvers

Louis J. Hinton

an advantage because of its soft workability when freshly quarried (it hardened after exposure to the air). According to Hinton, the sandstone could be cut (rather than pounded) into a specific shape and was much easier to work with than granite.

Perry never missed an opportunity to praise his carvers in his reports. He wrote, for example, that "The artistic workmen who have so lovingly wrought out the designs furnished them have surpassed their previous efforts in the way of good work and deserve high praise, if we do but remember how rare is the faculty they have displayed in these days of hurried competitive work."[6]

Some of the carvings were done from models carefully molded in advance and copied by the carvers with exactitude.

But this was not always the case. Hinton stated that much of the work was "carved without models, saving the state treasury a very considerable sum."[7] In the instances where the heads were of historical personages or actual living people, the models were made from photographs or paintings.

The Great Western Staircase is a gallery of great Americans, ranging from Washington, Jefferson, Hamilton, and Franklin to contemporary literary and political figures. The fact that the Civil War was still vivid in the nation's memory while the Capitol was being erected is abundantly exemplified in the carvings. Not only are the standard heroes of that conflict depicted in lifelike sculpture—Abraham Lincoln and Generals Grant, Sherman, and Sheridan—the staircase also enshrines John Brown, the abolitionist who advocated armed insurrection, and Frederick Douglass, who escaped from slavery to become a powerful abolitionist orator. The "Poets' Corner" includes Whitman, Longfellow, Whittier, and Bryant. Invention and science are personified in Robert Fulton and Joseph Henry. A prominent position is given to the portrait of J. V. L. Pruyn, an influential member of the original Capitol Commission.

The identities of a considerable number of the carvings are unknown, including a liberal sprinkling of children and a few elderly couples. Isaac Perry explained that "There are also many,

Frederick Douglass

A wild creature among carved leaves on the
Great Western Staircase

Great Western Staircase

were identified by the granddaughter herself, Lucretia Phelps, of Binghamton.

In 1897, complaints were heard that too many of the portraits were less historical than political and not worthy of being so honored. In response to this criticism, under Governor Frank Black's administration several were recarved.

About that time, too, someone realized that no historically important women had been included among the subjects. George W. Aldridge, the superintendent of public works whom Governor Black had assigned to finish the Capitol, hastily ordered the addition of six women: Molly Pitcher, the heroine who served as a soldier in the Revolution; Harriet Beecher Stowe, the author of *Uncle Tom's Cabin*; Susan B. Anthony, the suffragist leader; Clara Barton and Elmina P. Spencer, both Civil War nurses; and Frances E. Willard, the temperance crusader.

A final addition was the carving of corbels just beneath the skylight dome, with medallion profiles of all governors of New York State up through Frank Black. The portraits were designed by Louis Hinton. As for the governors, Perry explained, "Great care was taken to insure likeness in each case. Photos were obtained from authentic paintings of those who have passed beyond, those of our past Governors still with us were communicated with and kindly sent pictures that models

though smaller heads carved throughout the staircase that have been introduced for artistic effect, to vary the foliage wherever it was deemed suitable. They differ from the larger heads . . . in being merely decorative and not portraiture."[8] However, legend has persisted that the unidentified heads represent relatives or friends of the carvers. Two of the faces later turned out to be members of Perry's own family—his daughter Alice and granddaughter Lucretia. They were placed in separate locations but in the same corridor of the staircase, on the third level. They

Harriet Beecher Stowe and Susan B. Anthony

From left to right: Portrait of Lucretia Sexsmith, Isaac Perry's granddaughter;
profile portrait of Lucretia's mother, Alice Perry Sexsmith; to fill in spaces, artisans sometimes
carved faces of people who may have been members of their own families.

**Plaster model of
Robert Fulton**

were made from, for the carvers to copy. Blocks are left with space for six future Governors if posterity deems fit, as time rolls the meshes of his web, to have them carved therein."[9]

The workforce that created the Great Western Staircase was composed of stonecutters, stone carvers, stone setters, helpers, shed men, designers, and modelers. The employee time books in the Manuscripts Division of the New York State Library provide a glimpse of the hierarchy of the carvers. The foreman, Louis Hinton, directly supervised John Brines and Robert Walker in

Robert Fulton

the modeling. The carvers were then segregated by their pay, skill, and experience: Timothy Carey, P. Clune, Killian Drabold, and Louis Whittlesea were paid $5.00 a day; Thomas Dinkens, John Donaldson, Frank Sullivan, and John Noble were paid $4.50 a day; H. J. Walker earned $4.00 a day; and the remaining 52 carvers received 50 cents an hour for an eight-hour day.

The models for the historic portraits on the Great Western Staircase were crafted in the sheds on the east lawn of the Capitol, as well as by architectural sculptors in prominent studios in New York and Boston. The models were shipped to Albany, where they were placed on exhibit in the Capitol corridors pending their translation into stone. Records indicate that beginning in the 1880s the firms that supplied plaster models included Ellin and Kitson and the Palette Art Company of New York City, Evans and Tombs of Boston, and George Tolmie.

In the 1880s Charles M. A. Lange rose from the ranks as a Capitol painter to superintend the sculpture work and prepare models in 1893. Born in Albany in 1860, Lang studied at Cooper Union in New York and in Germany at the Munich Royal Academy. He became a sculptor, teacher, and a portrait artist. Included among the public figures that sat for portraits were Theodore Roosevelt, Governors David Hill and Roswell Flower, and John Wanamaker.

Another model maker for the Great Western Staircase was Otto Baumgartel. Trained as a wood carver in Germany, he arrived in New York City in 1885. He worked in the studio of Philip Martiny, a prominent architectural sculptor. Baumgartel may have also assisted in the sculpture for both the Grand Central and Pennsylvania railroad stations in New York City.

One of the chief stone carvers on the Great Western Staircase was Killian Drabold, then in his early thirties, who had moved his family from New York to Albany for the duration of the work. Born in Bavaria, Drabold was brought to America at the age of three. He immortalized his two young daughters by carving their puckish heads on either side of the dignified face of Amasa J. Parker, a justice of the New York State Supreme Court, congressman, and a power in the Democratic machine called the Albany Regency. Drabold may have also carved

Great Western Staircase, showing corbels yet to be carved

Carved corbels completed

William Cullen Bryant

Christopher Columbus, flanked by his ships

the stylistically similar portrait of Perry's little granddaughter Lucretia. A portrait of a young boy is said to represent Sanford Saxe, an unusually beautiful child who lived near the Capitol.

Among the other carvers under Hinton's supervision was a young man named John Francis Brines, who showed such

promise that Hinton brought him to the attention of Isaac Perry. After watching him work, Perry placed Brines in command of the carvers on the Eastern Approach and of designing and modeling its subjects.

John Brines came from Westerly, Rhode Island, where he had been born in 1860. At eighteen, he entered the studio of a celebrated sculptor, Carl H. Conrads, noted for statues of Alexander Hamilton in Central Park in New York and of General Sylvanus Thayer at West Point. Brines remained in Conrads's studio for six years. Brines and his wife lived for periods at the

Various historic scenes in the corbels.

Drawing of a stone carver at work in the Capitol,
Scribner's Monthly, December 1879

Clay model of Henry Hudson

One of the model makers was Otto R. Baumgartel, center, pictured in Philip Martiny's New York City studio. Left to right: George Wagner, artist; Philip Martiny, sculptor; Baumgartel; Adolph A. Weinman, sculptor and medalist; and an unidentified artist.

Gettysburg battlefield while he worked on a monument and at Hartford, Connecticut, where he did more carving. Brines was hired as a carver at the Albany Capitol in 1892 and became the chief designer and modeler on the Eastern Approach. When he took over that job, he remembered his out-of-work friends in Westerly and found places for them as carvers at the Capitol.

Brines spent eight years in Albany. He set up a studio in a shed on the grounds, where the designing and modeling were done for all the carvings on the terraced approach. In general, he picked the subjects himself, under Perry's watchful eye. Brines also contributed his model-making talent to the Great Western Staircase.[10] Among the models that Brines made were Poetry, Shakespeare, Milton, Longfellow, Faith, Hope, Charity, Fame, and Fortune.

Brines produced granite carvings of astonishingly fine detail. The white granite from Hallowell, Maine, being used on the Eastern Approach lent itself admirably to nuances of the chisel. The largest, most dazzling examples of intricate carving anywhere about the Capitol are the two almost-bacchanalian designs—Plenty and Progress—over the entrances to the porte-cochère that runs under the Eastern Approach and through which New York governors arrive at the Capitol.

Semicircular balconies jut out at the top of the staircase and are supported by 20-ton blocks of granite elaborately carved. The head of Jupiter is centered on one of these blocks, that of Mercury on the other. These were described by Perry as being "the largest pieces of granite carving in this country."[11]

Brines favored symbolism connected with American life and ideals, and he populated the staircase with personifications

Killian Drabold, a stone carver, working on Longfellow's beard

Life-size plaster models on display at the
Great Western Staircase, ca. 1890

Isaac Perry, center, and to his left John Francis Brines,
foreman of the carvers on the Eastern Approach

of liberty, literature, science, and art, as well as with a farmer, a mechanic, and a manufacturer. There are an Indian sachem and an eloquent head of a black man, representing emancipation of the slaves, with a chain about his chest with the middle link broken.

Perhaps Brines's choicest sculptures on the front staircase are indigenous American animals and birds—a wildcat, a raccoon, an owl, a raven, a wolf, a fox, a bison, a turkey, some eagles. Brines, like Hinton, preferred authentic models for his wildlife designs and would search for them accompanied by an assistant from his modeling shop, William G. Van Zant.

Van Zant recollected that "we sought to leave a permanent record of some of the animals and birds common to the earlier period of the country, and this state" (a notable exception to that aim is the head of a lion). Models were made in Brines's studio and then turned over to the carvers. Brines's other assistants were Charles Klinger of Albany and George Bonsette of Rome, Italy. Among carvers who worked on the Eastern Approach were Eugene Baldy, Richard Brines, and George Cruickshank.

When the Capitol was finished, John Brines and his wife traveled in Italy and France, and he studied for six months in Paris. Then he established a studio in New York creating sculpture of rare beauty. He died in 1905, of silicosis, at the age of forty-five.

Isaac Perry boasted of the carvings on the Eastern Approach that "the work has been done with the greatest care and precision and is superior to any other granite work in this country."[12]

Detail of balcony on Eastern Approach

Beast carved into the Eastern Staircase

The broken link in the chain symbolizes the emancipation of slaves.

Capitol, west facade, on March 29, 1911, the morning after the fire

CHAPTER THIRTEEN

OUT OF THE FLAMES

Franklin D. Roosevelt

THAT NIGHT LOUIS MCHENRY HOWE WORKED VERY LATE IN "PARK ROW," the third floor press rooms at the Capitol. He didn't mind the hour. As legislative correspondent for the *New York Telegram,* he was filing a story that was close to his heart.

The Democrats had won control of both houses of the Legislature for the 1911 session, and this automatically meant control by Tammany Hall. Louis Howe had been doing some part-time work for the reform Democrat Thomas Mott Osborne, trying to break the Tammany grip upstate. He knew it wasn't broken.

Soon after the 1911 session convened, a revolt flared among a small coterie of Democratic legislators. Their boyish leader was a freshman state senator out of Dutchess County; his name—soon to hit headlines from coast to coast—was Franklin Delano Roosevelt. Brashly, this youth with the Harvard profile and the pince-nez glasses pitted himself against the seasoned key men of Tammany at Albany—Alfred E. Smith, majority leader of the Assembly, and Robert F. Wagner, president pro tem of the Senate. Political suicide, everyone said.

At that time, United States Senators were elected not by direct vote of the people, but by state legislatures. The term of Chauncey M. Depew,

Louis McHenry Howe, seated, third from right

Republican, would expire in March. Naturally, the Legislature would choose a Democrat to succeed him. The Tammany boss, Charles F. Murphy, had picked his man—"Blue-Eyed Billy" Sheehan of Buffalo. Cynical newsmen, among them Louis Howe, poised their pencils to report the inevitable.

They as well as Murphy had done their reckoning without considering the new senator from Dutchess. Franklin Roosevelt gathered a score of Democratic insurgents to stand with him. They issued a manifesto that they would not support Sheehan and would not go along with any secret caucus. Their number was enough to block the election. The resulting deadlock went on for eleven weeks. Delightedly, Howe wrote: "It is the most humanly interesting political fight of many years."[1]

Day after day, the Legislature caucused, getting nowhere. Tempers shortened. Roosevelt gained more recruits. Howe's editor asked him to interview the young upstart. The reporter came away convinced that "nothing but an accident could keep him from becoming President of the United States."[2] This was

the beginning of the fateful relationship between Roosevelt and his "president-maker."

The night of Tuesday, March 28, the legislators held another fruitless caucus session in the Assembly Chamber. (Roosevelt and his group met at his Albany home, as usual.) Al Smith finally relieved Bob Wagner on the rostrum. The session dragged through four ballots until nearly 1 a.m. Weary members then retired to their hotel rooms. Two newsmen were still writing at 2:15 a.m.—Louis Howe, and Walter Arndt of the *New York Post*.

Dwight Goewey, proofreader for the Assembly, worked late for the same reason. It was past 2 o'clock when he went back to the Assembly library to close his desk and call it a night. The Assembly library doubled as a committee room for the Judiciary Committee. It opened off the east-west corridor leading to the rear entrance of the Assembly Chamber. As Goewey opened the door, a cloud of smoke greeted him, and dimly through it he saw flames licking up the bookshelves behind his desk. He slammed the door and ran all the way back through the Assembly Chamber and into the press rooms, yelling for a watchman. Howe and Arndt poked their heads out of their cubicles to ask "What's the trouble?" "There's a fire in the Assembly library," he replied, "and I'm afraid it may be a bad one."[3]

Neither newsman had the presence of mind to pick up a phone and report it, but both ran for the Assembly library, accompanied by H. S. Gorham, manager for Postal Telegraph in the Capitol. "We looked in the room," said Howe, "and saw the desk in the southwest corner ablaze. The fire at this time could have been easily put out with a pail or two of water. We searched in vain for anything to serve the purpose and finally decided to close the door and keep out the draft."[4]

In the nearby but separate State Library, which occupied the west portion of the third floor, the fire extinguishers had been freshly serviced, but the doors were locked. Because of the value of its contents, the library rules required that its own night watchman lock himself inside and make his periodic rounds. Somewhere within was that watchman, Sam Abbott, but he made no response to the commotion going on outside. A veteran of the Civil War, Abbott was seventy-eight years old and growing feeble; it was speculated that he may have dozed off in an upstairs guard room.

Goewey soon returned with Col. John Mullins, the only other night watchman on duty in the building. Mullins took a look and bolted down two long flights of stairs and outdoors to yank an alarm box in the street. It took 25 minutes for firemen to arrive and snake hose lines up the Great Western Staircase to the third floor.

Meanwhile, the Assembly library had become a furnace. Flames exploded through its glass transom and also through rear windows to leap catercorner across an airshaft into the State Library corridor. A wooden mezzanine that had been erected above the north portion of that corridor for extra book shelving took fire on the instant. The two newsmen beat a retreat to where the Senate corridor turns off at right angles and watched from there.

Until now, Albany Fire Chief William W. Bridgeford was confident of keeping the fire out of the State Library. The stone partition was thick between the corridor and the library, the only breach being the central door to the main reading room and a high row of window panes above it. Firemen played three streams into the wall of fire, expecting to confine it to the northern half of the corridor. Chief Bridgeford had Mullins go back downstairs and fetch an emergency key to the library. Mullins was fumbling with the key at the heavy oak door when a sheet of flame swept along the arched ceiling of the corridor. The high windowpanes burst, and a strong draft seemed to suck the flames into the library, where they leaped from shelf to shelf. The chief ordered his men to get inside the main reading room and work their way south, heading off the blaze. They tried to

West roof destroyed by fire

rush in, but heat scorched their hands so badly they couldn't hold onto the nozzles.

Once the fire had invaded the reading room, it was clear that the State Library would have to be written off. Its own carefully prepared firefighting apparatus was worthless. "The firemen confessed themselves helpless, and gave up any attempt to check the fiery advance."[5]

The two story reading room with its flanking stacks filled with books and magazines provided a perfect flue and the fuel to stoke it. Within 20 minutes, the blaze was shooting high through the roof. Scorched sheets of paper from the library were picked up six miles away, on the far side of the Hudson River, and kept as souvenirs.

By 4 o'clock in the morning, the State Library was an inferno, its precious contents having become a mass of fuel feeding one colossal flame towering high into the night sky. The entire city was illuminated by the eerie light, its populace awake and thronging to Capitol Hill.

As soon as the State Library was given up, the firemen's strategy shifted to saving the rest of the Capitol. If the flames had

ever captured one of the legislative chambers, Chief Bridgeford afterward said, the whole building would have gone. The Great Western Staircase, while offering a good vantage point for the firemen, was in particular jeopardy, being directly opposite the main entrance to the library. Before the night was over, the skylight over the stairs caved in and showered them with glass, some of it dripping, the molten glass like icicles. One firefighter exclaimed, "The very stones are burning."[6] Due to the excessive heat, some of the sandstone on the staircase literally melted. After the fire these sections of the staircase were replaced with newly carved sandstone.

The Senate Chamber never was seriously threatened; the Assembly Chamber was. At one point, flames crept into the attic space above the ceiling, and it began to burn. Firemen played high-pressure streams upon it from below, knocking out some of the papier-mâché coffers. The fire in the attic was doused—not without some further insult to the forgotten Hunt murals.

The famous papier-mâché panels, far from being flammable, were in fact fire resistant, and water absorbent, much more so than quartered oak would have been. And so the papier-mâché

State Library, reading room after the fire

State Library, main reading room, looking south, ca. 1895

was credited with saving the Assembly Chamber—and hence, perhaps, the whole Capitol. (Later, in the repair contract, 36 panels of the 396 were replaced.)

Both legislative chambers suffered water damage. The well of the Assembly Chamber became a lake. A member standing on its brink jokingly proposed a bill to stock it with fish. The Axminster carpeting was so sodden that stepping upon it was compared to walking on a bog. But the firefighters succeeded in confining the fire to the west section. Governor John A. Dix did business as usual next day in the Executive Chamber, bothered by nothing worse than a smoky smell.

In addition to the State Library and the bulk of its contents, many offices and committee rooms were destroyed, among them the sanctum of the Speaker of the Assembly. The southwest corner tower fell in, and several portions of the roof. The superb triangular wall of the Great Gable came through intact.

During the fire, Capitol employees began asking one another, "Has anyone seen Sam Abbott?" No one had. The old man was missing for two days. Then a cleanup squad found his charred body beneath rubbish in the fourth floor corridor. Apparently he had been trying to reach a door when overcome by smoke.

Next morning, the sun rose on a smoke-hazy, sleepy, and bewildered city. Just how much of the great building on the hill had been wrecked? Would it have to be entirely rebuilt?

The ruins smoldered, and fresh blazes broke out for days afterward. The building was placed under martial law, and National Guardsmen patrolled with rifles.

Albany's mayor offered the use of City Hall to the homeless Legislature. Uncomfortably, the Senate met in the city council chamber, the Assembly in the Supreme Court room. Al Smith made the motion to designate the city hall as temporary Capitol of New York State, and it passed. Then the lawmakers rushed through an appropriation of $100,000 with which to start the cleanup.

Black headlines shouted across the nation: STATE CAPITOL SWEPT BY FLAMES. Early estimates of the damage ran as high as $7 million. Incidentally, the state carried no insurance on the building. After sober appraisal, the state architect set the actual building damage at $1.6 million. The reconstruction work, in the end, cost well over $2 million.

Far beyond any monetary yardstick was the grievous loss sustained by the State Library. The fire was called the greatest library disaster of modern times. Flames devoured 450,000 books and 270,000 manuscripts. Many of the papers were priceless—such as early American colonial documents and the papers of statesmen. By luck and foresight, however, some of the rarest were saved. Commissioner of Education Andrew Sloan Draper—who had sounded repeated warnings of what a fire would do in the library stacks—had ordered certain items stored in a fireproof safe in the Regents' suite on the first floor. Among these were original drafts of Lincoln's Emancipation Proclamation and Washington's Farewell Address, also the "spy papers" that Major John André had concealed in his boot when captured after his rendezvous with Benedict Arnold. The fire was confined to the third floor and above.

Too long to be accommodated in this safe had been a dress sword that once belonged to George Washington. The sword was stored in a library closet and was bemoaned as lost in the fire. After several days, the sword was found, considerably damaged, beneath a thick pile of charred books. It was straightened out.

Great Western Staircase, fourth floor after the fire

Sandstone columns melted by the fire

The 1911 annual report of the State Library recognized the library staff for saving books and manuscripts after the fire. They had "endured cold, wet and smoke for days." "On their own initiative," the "heads of different sections of the Library, and others for two weeks did the work of laborers, which no one else had the requisite knowledge of books and locations to do so well." "Especially difficult and indeed dramatic," the report continued, "was the work done in saving manuscripts in the first forty-eight hours after the fire."[7]

The staggering irony was that the State Library was just marking time before moving into its new quarters in the State Education Building across the street. That building was completed the following year, far behind schedule.

Generous offers of books to restore the State Library poured in. One such helping hand was extended by the Parliamentary Library in Ottawa—housed in a Thomas Fuller building. Sardonic coincidence may be read into the fact that the three major governmental structures that Fuller designed (at least in part) on the American continent were visited by catastrophe. San Fran-

cisco City Hall was reduced to rubble by the earthquake of 1906. The main Parliament building at Ottawa was burned in 1916 in a mysterious fire widely blamed on German sabotage, in which several people perished.

Salvage operations commencing after the fire

Reading room

West facade after the fire

What caused the Capitol fire at Albany? The question never was answered with finality. Gossip whispered that some legislator, after the late caucus, dropped a cigar butt into a wastebasket. But the caucus was held in the Assembly Chamber proper, not the Assembly library. Another rumor said a watchman had reported just recently that a light switch was heating up and that nothing was done about it. This was not verified.

The likeliest explanation is that the electrical system was still functioning with the primitive wiring installed twenty-five years before, when electric lights were a novelty. More than once, appropriations for new wiring had been refused. There was an immediate inspection of the wiring, and it was found to be "very defective." Insulation was worn through; wires had been laid against bare wood; telephone and bell-signal wires were found in contact with light wires. If a short circuit hadn't occurred yet, it was a miracle. Without waiting for legislative approval, Governor Dix ordered the old wires yanked out and an emergency wiring system put in. No time was wasted, either, in installing fire extinguishers and standpipes.

The fire had its political impact, too. Unquestionably, it hastened the end of the senatorial deadlock. The Legislature was cramped and unhappy in City Hall. It wanted to go home while its own chambers were put in order. Murphy, the Tammany sachem, caught a train for Albany. He proposed a compromise candidate, James A. O'Gorman, a Supreme Court justice. Most of the insurgents capitulated. O'Gorman was elected U. S. Senator on the 63rd caucus ballot, on March 31. Franklin D. Roosevelt, with two other holdouts, stayed away from the caucus.

The Legislature then adjourned for two weeks. When it reconvened on April 17, the damaged corridors were boarded up and both Chambers were habitable, though Assemblymen complained that the very walls oozed dampness. Nearly every member was lacking his ready file of bills; they had been drenched and ruined the night of the fire. The first action in both Houses was to transfer the Capitol of New York State from City Hall back to where it belonged.

The area of the State Library (which would begin life anew in the Education Building) was converted into the Legislative Library, merging the Senate and Assembly libraries into one. The main reading room was only one story in height to accommodate new office space on the fourth floor level above.

The design for the Legislative Library was begun under State Architect Franklin B. Ware in May 1912. Ware designed the Capitol's interior after the 1911 fire using principles of the École des Beaux Arts. The chaotic accretion of divided corridors and cubicles that preceded the fire was replaced by offices, corridors, and committee rooms that flanked the library. Completed by State Architect Lewis Pilcher, the Legislative Library had Vermont white marble walls, columns, capitals, and cornices that were richly carved. A series of murals by Will H. Low formed a frieze along three sides of the rooms. They reflect the American Renaissance movement and contain allegorical figures

Papers and books from library collections
scattered along State Street

Papier-mâché panel from ceiling
of the Assembly Chamber

Architectural models for the Legislative Library
produced by Joseph Smith & Company of New York

Wood scaffolding on the western half of the Capitol during reconstruction

state government continued to expand, additional office space was needed. In 1943, Governor Thomas E. Dewey launched the most sweeping program of interior alterations. Mezzanines were constructed; ceilings were lowered to accommodate heating and ventilating systems; gracefully proportioned rooms and corridors were subdivided; and original glass transoms were blocked.

Legislative Library

Legislative Library, showing the seal of
New York State carved into the fireplace

representing commerce, agriculture, civilization, art, literature, science, liberty, record, study, thrift, suffrage, law, civic force, justice, manufacture, and transportation.

The only exterior change resulting from the fire was the addition of three small dormers on either side of the Great Gable.

The original plan of the Capitol had included rooms for the executive, legislative, and judicial branches of government. As

Legislative Library, Will H. Low, mural panel

Much of the Capitol's original ornamentation was hidden by these "improvements." The skylights that had filtered at least some natural light into the stairwells of the Assembly and Senate staircases were eliminated when a corridor and newly created offices were installed in those spaces.

Now and again, when workmen took up their tools to cut an opening in a wall, they would be confronted by a formidable rampart of solid granite several feet thick. It would take days to drill through.

Those who planned and promoted the Capitol had been public-spirited, high-minded, conscientious men. They were not third-rate politicians dreaming up a boondoggle. They had a vision. They intended a majestic, inspired edifice that would shout to the world the wealth and importance of the Empire State. The time was ripe for such an enterprise, with the nation's industry expanding and its economy booming in the wake of the Civil War. Who worried about the money to push railroads to the Pacific Coast? Americans were thinking and talking big.

Considering the vicissitudes of its gestation, the wonder is that the New York Capitol turned out as well as it did. As was remarked at the outset, it probably is without peer as a building in which architecture and politics are intermingled. It is an essay in stone on the American democratic system, which is far from perfect but the best yet devised, in which the hopes and ideals have a way of coming out on top of the mistakes and fumblings.

The architects expected the Capitol to be surrounded by spacious, well-tended grounds. The plan was to demolish adjacent residential buildings so that a spectator might stand off and appreciate its facades from a distance, as they might observe a painting in a gallery. Frederick Law Olmsted's successor firm prepared a simple landscape plan for East Capitol Park that was only partially implemented. The Capitol was hemmed in by blocks of row houses to the west, north, and south.

A full century after the preliminary legislation that set it going, the New York Capitol found itself the pivot of a far greater development than was envisioned by its early sponsors in their most optimistic moments. Like the elder statesman, mellow in years and wisdom, it was elected to preside at the head of the South Mall—the future working heart of New York State government. The South Mall—later rechristened the Governor Nelson A. Rockefeller Empire State Plaza—would place the Capitol in its true and rightful perspective for the first time since it was built.

Demolition of houses adjacent to the Capitol, ca. 1964

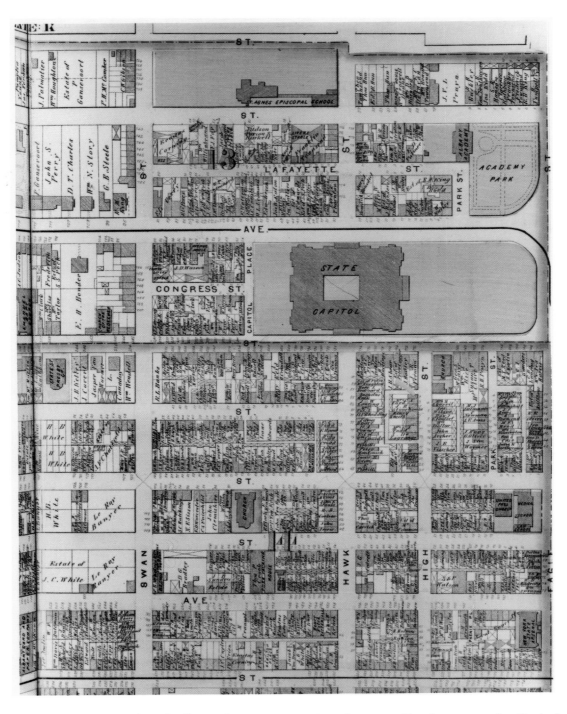

Map from an 1876 atlas of Albany showing proximity of surrounding houses to the Capitol

Empire State Plaza at night

CHAPTER FOURTEEN

THE EMPIRE STATE PLAZA

Empire State Plaza

A REPORTER AT A PRESS BRIEFING ONCE ASKED GOVERNOR NELSON A. Rockefeller if it was correct to refer to him as a frustrated architect. The governor gestured toward the great south windows of the Red Room and replied "not anymore." In a speech on another occasion he noted that he might indeed have an "edifice complex." It is a fact that Rockefeller, while a student at Dartmouth, seriously contemplated architecture as a career.

The governor's allusions were to the complex of marbled buildings known as the South Mall during much of its creation, but rechristened by Rockefeller himself as the Empire State Plaza. Not long before his death that name was expanded by Governor Hugh L. Carey to the Governor Nelson A. Rockefeller Empire State Plaza. It rears resplendently as the tangible symbol of his governorship. No other chief executive of the state of New York left so prodigious an imprint on the face of the capital city.

The principal architect, Wallace K. Harrison, of Harrison and Abramovitz, declared that the Plaza was an extension of the Capitol. This was how Rockefeller regarded it, although the style of architecture was drastically different. Far from downgrading the Capitol, the extravagant new complex of governmental structures complements and enshrines it. The massive, century-old building has been brought into true focus as it never was before, particularly when viewed from the south end of the Plaza along the line of reflecting pools and framed by tall marble buildings.

One of the early things Rockefeller did as governor was to ask for a complete tour of the Capitol. He was fascinated by the building and often roamed its corridors to study architectural details—the legislative chambers, the superb stairways, the profuse carvings. He mentioned to his secretary, Dr. William J. Ronan, that a book should be done on the history and the intriguing architecture of the Capitol, and set his staff photographer to taking pictures around the building. Such was the genesis of this book's first edition. Rockefeller felt that the much-maligned Capitol ought to be rehabilitated and take its rightful place in any future state plans. By his order, the grounds were improved with floriculture, a fountain, and the removal of dying trees. The east facade was floodlit at night.

Nelson Aldrich Rockefeller was not only the wealthiest of all New York's governors. With the single exception of George

Color postcard view of Albany south of the Capitol, future site of the South Mall, now the Governor Nelson A. Rockefeller Empire State Plaza

Clinton, the first governor, Rockefeller established a record for tenure in the office—15 years and election to four terms. During most of those years he was directly involved with erecting the South Mall. He was able to watch its progress day by day from his office windows, and he frequently donned a hard hat to inspect the working areas. It was his obsession. He stated his philosophy on the project in this fashion: "Mean structures breed small vision. But great architecture reflects mankind at its true worth. [The Mall] should fulfill us aesthetically as well as serve us practically."[1]

Rockefeller had come to Albany with no preconceived notion of making over the capital city, with which he was scarcely familiar. But fresh in his memory were visits to Brazil's spectacular new capital, Brasilia, by which he was much impressed. Upon moving into the Executive Mansion on Eagle Street in January 1959, he was taken aback at the unkempt, down-at-heels aspect of the nearby streets verging on the South End slums. The realization that his family had become residents of a badly deteriorated inner city went against his aesthetic grain. Soon the new governor became aware of a related problem— namely, a severe shortage of space for the needs of state government. Rentals were being paid for state offices scattered in at least 10 commercial buildings around the city.

Talking with his budget director, T. Norman Hurd, Rockefeller learned that there was additional office space available at the State Campus, a spread of 12 office buildings three miles west of downtown Albany, a plan for which had been formulated under Governor Thomas E. Dewey as a hoped-for solution to the space dilemma. (That development, pushed through by Governor Averell Harriman in the 1950s, had no connection with the campus of the State University at Albany later constructed a little farther west). Harriman voiced doubt as to the wisdom of moving so many state units to the outskirts. Those doubts were echoed by the downtown merchants.

An episode that had an incidental bearing on Rockefeller's reaction to Albany during his first year in office was a visit by Princess Beatrix of The Netherlands. The state was holding a Hudson-Champlain Celebration in 1959, marking the 350th anniversary of the exploratory voyages of Henry Hudson and Samuel de Champlain. Holland sent her twenty-one-year-old

Demolition for the South Mall, 1966

princess as official delegate to the former Dutch colony. A motor tour of historic places up the Hudson Valley was climaxed at the city of Hudson where Beatrix boarded Laurance Rockefeller's yacht *Dauntless,* to enter Albany by water as Henry Hudson's *Half-Moon* had done. The princess was landed at the foot of Madison Avenue, where she was met by Mrs. Nelson Rockefeller and their daughter Mary, and whisked to the Executive Mansion on Eagle Street by the governor's limousine. Nelson himself was in New York City that day, meeting with the Soviet premier, Nikita Khrushchev, but returned to play the gracious host to Princess Beatrix at the Mansion. The governor afterward admitted to embarrassment at having a royal guest see some decrepit samples of the capital city, and the press made a considerable point of this, but it was by no means crucial in triggering the South Mall.

Rockefeller learned that Albany's Democratic mayor, Erastus Corning 2nd, was allied with a group of business leaders in urging a joint state-city effort to salvage the ailing downtown. The governor, by executive order, called a halt to further construction at the State Campus. At his behest, in March 1961 the legislature created a Temporary State Commission on the Capital City, headed by Lieutenant Governor Malcolm Wilson. Rockefeller had already decided that the ideal solution would be to combine the twin objectives of more space and the resuscitation of the Albany center.

The Wilson commission produced a report in January 1962, recommending that the state

concentrate all future building in the heart of the city. Of several potential locations, it favored a "South Mall" along a north-south axis extending from the Capitol nearly to the Executive Mansion, between State Street and Madison Avenue. Not only would this site be handy to the existing state complex on Capitol Hill, but its elevation would make a dramatic skyline.

The commission submitted a map showing boundaries of the tract to be taken by the state under right of eminent domain. The tract embraced 40 city blocks, plus a right-of-way for arterial highway approaches and ramps down to the river, and a narrow strip along the riverfront to accommodate pump houses for the use of Hudson River water in the huge air-conditioning system. The total area came to 98.5 acres. The 40-block tract contained 3,300 dwelling units, 350 business establishments, and a population of 6,800. It was predominantly residential, with three story brownstone and brick row houses dating as far back as the early nineteenth century. Neighborhoods in decline, but not (as often asserted) a part of the vice-ridden Albany "Gut," notorious for its bordellos and winos.

The South Mall proposal was kept under wraps as long as feasible, to guard against land speculators moving in and buying properties cheaply. The governor asked for $20 million in his deficiency budget to cover acquisition of the parcels to be condemned. By the end of January 1962, the Legislature had given the go-ahead signal by approving the deficiency budget including this sum. No statute specifically authorizing the construction of the South

**Model of the South Mall with a memorial arch
at the southern terminus, 1963**

Mall was legislated. Instead, the Legislature—in a mood to give Rockefeller anything he asked—sanctioned the project by voting appropriations for it as budgetary items.

At this juncture Mayor Corning was invited over to the Capitol, informed of the plan, and shown the map. The mayor went back to City Hall and dictated a letter of protest to the commission, saying its proposal would violate "human rights"[2] and deprive the city of about $500,000 in realty taxes per year. Ignoring this remonstrance, the machinery of eminent domain ground steadily forward. By the governor's order, on March 27, 1962, the State Department of Public Works filed with the Department of State and the Albany County Clerk maps of the tract the state was appropriating. With that, Mayor Corning fired off a yet stronger letter to Rockefeller, charging "ruthless misuse of power by the Executive"[3] and "what might be expected of a dictatorship." As the final touch, he wrote: "Do not build this magnificent monument on a foundation of human misery."[4]

The aristocratic Albany mayor backed up his words with legal action. The city filed for an injunction to prevent seizure of the properties and on April 4 was granted a temporary stay by a judge of the State Supreme Court. The State appealed, and the Appellate Division reversed the lower court's ruling on June 29. Corning, having made his point, carried the appeal no farther. On the contrary, after Rockefeller's reelection sweep, the mayor swung over into a cooperative role, recognizing that the South Mall would be beneficial to the city. Corning afterward explained that he had begun the action because he was concerned about the State's taking the streets as well as the blocks. The plan was changed to leave the streets to the city for maintenance of water, sewer, lighting, and cleaning.

Having cleared the way for South Mall construction, in July 1962 Rockefeller mounted the operator's seat of a giant crane and aimed a steel clam shovel against one of the doomed buildings. By this act, he symbolically touched off one of the largest, most complicated, and costly single construction projects in history. All down the line, he repeatedly proclaimed that the South Mall would make Albany one of the most beautiful and spectacular capitals in the world.

Now Rockefeller found his opportunity to be allied for the final and climactic time with Wallace Harrison, an eminent

**Governor Nelson A. Rockefeller unveiling
a model of the South Mall, 1963**

**Governor Rockefeller and Mayor Erastus Corning 2nd at the
demolition of the Ten Eyck Hotel, 1970**

New York architect and personal friend of long standing. When he became Assistant Secretary of State for Latin American Affairs during World War II, Rockefeller had called Harrison to Washington and made him coordinator, with special reference to cultural relations. Their close association dated from the 1930s when Wally Harrison designed Rockefeller Center and the Radio City Music Hall for John D. Rockefeller Jr., who appointed his son Nelson as president of the Center. Harrison had since been the principal architect on such noted structures as the United Nations building and the Metropolitan Opera House in Lincoln Center, and had built a private mansion for Nelson on the family estate at Pocantico Hills.

On a flight together from Washington to New York, Rockefeller told Harrison about the planned Albany Mall and, on the back of an envelope, sketched his rough notion of what it should be. Harrison tossed in ideas of his own. Not surprisingly, when the time came, the firm of Harrison and Abramovitz received the contract as chief architect for the South Mall. Before the job was done, six architectural firms were involved. Most notably, James and Meadows and Howard, of Buffalo, designed the Legislative Office Building; Sargent, Webster, Crenshaw and Folley, of Syracuse, was selected for the Justice Building; and Carson, Lundin, and Shaw, of New York City, was responsible for the motor vehicle building. The total architectural and engineering fees were $37.8 million, of which the Harrison firm's share was $10.1 million.

As yet, however, no financial prescription for the South Mall had been worked out. Rockefeller was not so politically naive as to imagine that the voters would approve a bond issue of the necessary dimensions in a referendum. The first published estimate of the cost was $400 million—about as realistic as the initial $4 million limit for the Capitol had been. It is uncanny how, on a hugely magnified scale, the Capitol's history was repeated in the building of the South Mall—in the ballooning cost, the constantly lengthening time schedule, and the barrage of criticism.

While the demolition was going on, Mayor Corning performed so complete an about-face that he came to the aid of the South Mall and earned the title of its "financial architect." He called on Governor Rockefeller to propose a lease-purchase formula by which the city of Albany would employ its credit in floating municipal bonds to defray the construction costs; the city, as technical owner, would then lease the buildings to the state. The state's annual rental payments would be applied to the principal, while also meeting the carrying costs of the bonds. With the final payment in the year 2004, if not before, the Mall would become the property of the state. Rockefeller "went for the plan like a trout for a fly,"[5] to quote Corning, an ardent fisherman. The mayor afterward said, "It was a tremendously tricky arrangement, and lots of lawyers worked on it."[6] Some referred to it as "backdoor financing." In January 1964, at Corning's suggestion, the method was amended so that Albany County, instead of the city, issued the bonds.

The Wilson Commission had also recommended that the Capitol be given an external cleaning for the first time since it was erected. The big scrub-down was done in 1966 with a combination of steam and chemicals. The public had come to accept the unsightly coating of grime as the Capitol's normal hue. People were agreeably surprised as the pristine off-white beauty of the Maine granite was revealed. The cosmetic treatment spruced up the Capitol for its coming marriage with the South Mall.

Governor Rockefeller inspecting the construction site, 1967

With announcement of the financing formula, a scale model of the architectural dream was unveiled in the east lobby of the Capitol. A feature of the model was an Arch of Freedom thrusting skyward at the south extreme of the Mall, facing the Capitol. But the governor sensed that the arch would be a weak southern terminus for the giant Plaza, as if it were dwindling away into nowhere. It was replaced by the Cultural Education Center, a far more effective counterweight to the Capitol.

As the old buildings were being obliterated, powdered plaster drifted across Capitol Hill like a smokescreen. Excavation followed, and streets and sidewalks were alternately muddy and dusty. The Mall ran into the same initial problem as the Capitol—the deep deposit of glutinous blue clay streaked with sand that had to be removed. In all, 3,124,000 cubic yards of earth were excavated. This basic task in itself served notice that the South Mall job was not going to be accomplished thriftily. The foundations took twice as long and cost twice as much as the original estimate.

Digging was followed by pile driving, a procedure that shattered the calm of Capitol Hill for more than five years. The

Agency Buildings under construction, looking west

decibels of this assault upon the eardrums of state workers and nearby residents were a reminder of the engineering strides that had been taken since the Capitol was built. As many as 26,000 H-shaped steel pilings were driven as foundation supports to an average depth of 70 feet to get into glacial gravel underlying the clay. In addition, around the rectangular perimeter of the Mall area were driven 20,000 tons of interlocked steel sheet pilings for cofferdams—to preserve the normal water table in the ground outside the foundations.

Long before the South Mall had been envisioned, Rockefeller had established the Office of General Services in 1960, appointing as its first commissioner General Cortlandt van Rensselaer Schuyler. Schuyler had been chief U.S. military representative on the Allied Control Commission for Romania at the end of World War II, and the Pentagon had later assigned him to Rockefeller's staff in Washington. Construction of the South Mall was at first under jurisdiction of the Department of Public Works, while the Office of General Services had charge of overall planning and design. Before long, Rockefeller transferred supervision of the whole job to General Schuyler and the Office of General Services. Schuyler needed a coordinator and Dr. Ronan recommended Brigadier General William W. Wanamaker, at that time with the State University of New York Construction Authority. In this way Wanamaker became the initial director of Mall construction. But in the last analysis no one could dispute that the real boss was Nelson Rockefeller.

Now that the die was cast, the first critical decision to be made was what kind of stone to use. The choice fell upon marble as being the most economical, as well as attractive and abundant. The bulk of the marble for the Mall was to come from Vermont and Georgia, some from Alabama, and in one instance from Greece. The Grecian verde tinos serpentine was used on the floor and columns of the tall, spacious central lobby of the Legislative Office Building. For several years the Albany Mall was to devour nearly the entire output of Vermont marble; indeed, one Rutland quarry was depleted. Other varieties of stone were used, here and there, including granites for some paving and stairways. In the latter category, a considerable amount of the relatively rare dark grey igneous rock meta-anorthosite was obtained from an Adirondack quarry at Upper Jay. Because

**Construction of Corning Tower, Agency Buildings (center),
and framing for the Legislative Office Building (foreground), 1969**

Harrison wanted touches of darker stone for contrast with the glaring whiteness of all the marble, a quantity of brownish sandstone called Llenroc (Cornell spelled backward) came from a quarry near Ithaca. Its use is noteworthy in the eastern wall and parapet of the Plaza and in the lower part of the Cultural Education Center.

The architectural plan crystallized down to 12 buildings. The pivotal "topmast" of the complex is the Tower Building, 589 feet high, the tallest skyscraper in the state north of Manhattan. The others, ranged about the quarter-mile-long plaza are the four Agency (office) buildings, the Legislative Office Building, the Justice Building, the Cultural Education Center, the Performing Arts Center (commonly known as "The Egg"), the Swan Street Building (Motor Vehicles Department), a low res-

taurant building beside the Tower, and the Platform Building. The last named is the largest—in fact one of the biggest in the world—but the casual visitor would hardly sense its existence because it is mainly underground. Most of the other major buildings rest upon it.

The bubbling enthusiasm of Rockefeller could not wait for the actual "laying" of a cornerstone. Instead, he unveiled one. On June 21, 1965—barely two months after disclosing the financial plan—he staged the unveiling ceremony on a plank platform near the northwest corner of the Swan Street Building, for which only a fragment of the foundation was yet complete. The carefully chosen stone, to be mortared in place at a later date, was a 7,500 pound block of white granite quarried at Concord, New Hampshire—an obvious symbol of the Capitol connection.

Aerial view of "the Egg" under construction

Swan Street Building, 1970

Beaming broadly as he dropped the covering, Rockefeller hailed the event as beginning "Albany's transformation into one of the most brilliant, beautiful, efficient, and electrifying capitals in all the world."[7] He then filled a document box that was to be sealed into a slot behind the cornerstone. As a copy of the financial agreement was handed to him for deposit, he quipped, with a grin at Mayor Corning: "Handle that with care. It took us a year and a half to draw it up."[8]

The same day a release from the governor's office deferred the Mall's estimated completion date from 1970 to 1972 and hinted that the $400 million cost might creep upward by as much as $100 million.

The Swan Street building was the first to be occupied, in 1971. It is five blocks (1,200 feet) long, with two porticos for breaks between segments. This stretched-out structure was purposely designed with a low profile, making it a transitional step between the Mall towers and the ranks of brick townhouses across the street. The massive granite cornerstone today faces Swan Street with large deep-carved letters: SOUTH MALL.

The South Mall project was plagued with problems from its inception. Among the first to rear its head was an acute shortage of labor in the capital area, especially of carpenters and pile drivers. Many workers were brought in from New York City and Montreal, and this bred discontent among local unions. Wage scales escalated. When a bearded young Canadian worker called "Frenchy" quit to return to Montreal, his compatriots gave him a farewell party with the toast: "Here's to the project that never ends!"[9] The work force at maximum numbered over 3,000. Wildcat strikes, slowdowns, and featherbedding multiplied. In one year, 1970, labor disputes totaled 217.

Of greater import was the hurried, almost impetuous way in which primary contracts were let. At the outset, while he had a compliant legislature, Rockefeller got funds committed so if political winds shifted work would go on. The Capitol was an object lesson in this respect. Another factor spurring him on was the certainty of inflating costs as time passed. Behind it all, however, was the impatient driving force of the governor. The state signed six major contracts almost simultaneously, stipulating the approximate starting date for all, when each depended, in some degree, upon the completion of one preceding. A consequence

was that at times workmen were fairly tripping over one another.

In retrospect, General Schuyler frankly avowed, the Mall would have been erected in a more orderly manner had it not been pushed so fast in the beginning. The difficulties began, according to Schuyler, when the contractor on the foundation fell behind schedule, thereby delaying the others. At the peak of construction, 359 contractors and sub-contractors were on site at one time. By 1970 the South Mall was running three years behind schedule, and Schuyler publicly admitted that the state was largely responsible for the delays. "There was more complexity to the project then we realized," he said.[10] To keep contractors from suing in the Court of Claims for losses due to improper planning, a number of "equitable adjustments" costing millions were made.

The original contract figure for the five-level Platform Building was $97,777,000, and the job was so gigantic that it was shared by two New York City contractors. It proved the classic instance of cost overruns. Before it was finished, the Waish-Corbetta combine, alleging that the State had not properly coordinated and scheduled the work, was awarded without contest an additional $49,725,971, bringing the total contract value to $149,750,000. The enormity of the Platform Building may be appreciated by reflecting that it contains the Grand Concourse extending the length of the mall beneath the Plaza; the Convention Center, whose main room, unobstructed by pillars, will accommodate 2,700 people and has six meeting rooms besides; four levels of the State Health Department's laboratories; a bus terminal and underground parking spaces for 3,000 cars, along with the various utilities installations.

Cost estimates for the Mall were revised upward year by year. The Democratic state comptroller, Arthur Levitt, predicted that the figure would escalate to at least a billion. In 1968, Levitt sent a letter to both houses of the Legislature asking for an investigation into the soaring costs, referring to the Mall as "an insatiable project." Rockefeller revealed how stung he was by Levitt's attacks by going before the Legislature with a special message in reply. He acknowledged that the pricetag had recently been increased from $480 million to $610 million but reminded the legislators that extending the construction period over still more years could only result in far higher costs. The governor wound

Empire State Plaza, aerial view

up his eloquent defense by heaping praise on the Legislature for its "continued support" and its "great vision."[11]

By 1971 the cost estimate was up to $850 million. By 1975 the total of Mall bonds authorized by Albany County was $985 million. In 1976, Levitt proclaimed that the lease and interest payments would boost the total past $2 billion. Actually, the more accurate final figure, including rental and carrying costs, turned out to be around $1.7 billion.

History was repeated in the torrent of ridicule that fell upon the architecture long before the project was completed. The more strident of its critics called it such things as "a naive hodgepodge of barely digested design ideas,"[12] "a compendium of clichés of modern architecture,"[13] and "Buck Rogers creating a seat of government."[14] Others wrote that "Stylistically, the Albany Mall leaves one not knowing whether to laugh or cry,"[15] or "Its characteristics are pomposity and banality,"[16] or "Reality is in short supply in this complex."[17]

The Mall had its defenders as well—generally less vocal, as had been the case with the Capitol. They maintained that "its roots were aesthetic"[18] and hailed it as "an artistic triumph."[19] The chief architect, Wallace Harrison, took the brickbats in stride. With him it was an old story. Time would bring acceptance and approval. Shortly before his death (in 1981), he commented that there was no better governmental complex anywhere else in the world. Under sharp questioning in the Senate hearings for his appointment as U.S. vice president, Rockefeller gamely defended the Mall project, observing that similar statements were made about Rockefeller Center.

While the Tower was rising to its 44 stories in height, the cranes operating on its summit were a long-term spectacle on Albany's skyline. Twice during its construction fires flared through its upper levels. One workman was killed in a fall down an elevator shaft. The lofty structure is faced with more marble than the United Nations building, and its windows contain a million dollars worth of glass. The observation deck comprising its 42nd floor affords a stunning panorama. The Tower looks down upon the row of four identical 19 story Agency Buildings on the opposite side of the reflecting pools. In Harrison's view, this Plaza, which was the crown of his long artistic career, "is the only place I know of where skyscrapers are used with space around them so everybody can enjoy the light and air."

At the time the Plaza was being designed, the State Department of Health, then quartered on Holland Avenue, was petitioning for a new laboratory building in the vicinity of the Albany Medical Center. Rockefeller seized the opportunity to entice a major state operating department into the Mall. He offered the health commissioner, Dr. Hollis Ingraham, the option of waiting years for the money to build a new laboratory or moving downtown into the Tower building. The result was a drastic change in design planning for the Tower.

The four subsurface levels in the Platform Building beneath the Tower were set apart for the laboratories, while the departmental offices were assigned the first 14 floors of the Tower. The move gave the Health Department the enviable good fortune of acquiring the most advanced of laboratory equipment while developing, in collaboration with the architect, fail-safe controls over all laboratory processes. Consequently the laboratory became a building within a building. Harrison worked long hours with the lab staff, planning the ambience down to the finest details, even to the colors of paint on the walls.

A latecomer to the South Mall plan, the Cultural Education Center was the happiest thought of the entire complex.

First called the Museum-Library Building, it eventuated as the shared domicile of the State Museum, the State Library, and the State Archives. The contract for its construction was let in 1969. Architecturally, it is regarded as the jewel of the Plaza, and Harrison himself considered it his best contribution. Characterized by distinctly separated layers with vertical window slots, it flares outward toward the top with a faint resemblance to a pagoda.

The strongest reason for so substantial a building at the south end of the Mall, instead of a frivolous arch, was the severely overstrained condition of the State Library after a half-century in the pillared Education Building following the disastrous Capitol fire of 1911. Everyone mourned the evacuation of the magnificent reading room and rotunda created by Henry Hornbostel, but books were being piled in stack corridors and overflow resources stored in an outlying warehouse. The new reading room is purely utilitarian, with no vaulted ceiling and no tall ornate windows, but the well-ventilated stacks beneath occupy entire floors and allow for future expansion of contents by millions of volumes. The library has 77 miles of shelving.

The State Museum occupying the lower floors of the Cultural Education Center took the opportunity to create an entirely new museum environment, employing the latest museum techniques. The exhibits were developed around the theme of "Man and His Environment."

Governor Rockefeller had never felt comfortable with the South Mall name. It reminded him too much of a shopping center. On November 21, 1973, he presided over a dedication ceremony with which he formally rechristened it the Empire State Plaza. Crane booms were still swinging, air compressors chugging, and a bitter wind blew. A knot of spectators gathered around a massive block of polished Brazilian granite on which were graven the words: EMPIRE STATE PLAZA—DEDICATED TO THE PEOPLE OF NEW YORK. This monument stands at the north end of the Plaza, nearest the Capitol. Speculation as to the reason for this unseasonable event was confirmed on December 11 when Rockefeller announced he would resign the governorship to pursue "a new national role,"[20] saying he felt he had accomplished all he could as governor. Malcolm Wilson moved up to governor, and in February 1974 he appointed his former superior as chairman of a Citizens Advisory Committee on the Empire State Plaza with duties of "guidance and suggestions."

The most controversial structure in the Plaza is the oddly shaped Performing Arts Center, commonly referred to as "The Egg." It has been variously compared to half a grapefruit, to a watermelon cut on a bias, or a radar disc with a lid. Instead of marble, its material is concrete. There is not a straight line in the whole structure; even two of the elevators are round. The shape is somewhat elliptical—more precisely an oblate spheroid. To John C. Byron, it was "the biggest headache of all." Byron was director of construction from 1971 until the Empire State Plaza was finished. The reason for the extraordinary difficulties was that The Egg was a totally new construction form, with no engineering precedent. An exact model was first built for study and experiment. A computer was used to calculate curvatures and stresses. Concrete pouring was a ticklish problem because of the curving wooden forms and differing thicknesses of the walls. Because concrete generates heat as it hardens, ice cubes were mixed with some pourings to ensure uniform curing.[21]

The nickname The Egg was hatched as a jocular term among engineers and hardhats working on its construction. A

Governor Rockefeller delivering a speech at the dedication of the Empire State Plaza, 1973

public relations agency promoting its formal opening in May 1978 picked up the catchword and made it endure. The label was distasteful to many, including Rockefeller and his architect, but, once embedded in the vernacular, impossible to eradicate. Harrison took the Shakespearean attitude that "a rose by any other name would smell as sweet." The sobriquet, at all events, did not hinder the building's flowering into an entertainment center.

Much as The Egg has been deprecated by critics, it provides a striking counterpoint to the austere vertical lines of the Tower and the Agency buildings. Perched atop a slim concrete pedestal, it leaves open vistas of the Hudson River and the hills beyond that a conventional structure would have blocked off.

A Meeting Hall, spacious enough to accommodate 1,500 guests at dinner, was quietly added to the Plaza's design in 1965 beneath the future site of The Egg. This eliminated the need for a convention hall in Albany as had been recommended by the Commission on the Capital City.

The Grand Concourse (the adjective has been dropped) is walled with travertine from Italy. It evolved into far more than a passageway between buildings. Lined with a variety of stores, branch banks, restaurants, and cafeterias, it functions as a subsidiary shopping center for state workers. Its midline spaces are frequently utilized for special exhibits and trade shows. The Concourse also serves as a remarkable art gallery.

Ornamental aspects of the open air Plaza itself were well provided for in advance. For example, as early as 1967 a nursery was contracted to begin growing 576 trees for the final cosmetic touch when the Plaza was completed. Little saplings were planted and grew "faster than the Mall." By 1975 the maples were 20 feet high and fears were heard that they might grow too big to be moved. The worry proved groundless. Transplanted in neat rows along either side of the reflecting pools and fountains, the trees and shrubs were trimmed in cubic forms to harmonize with the buildings. In winter, the reflecting pool adjacent to the Capitol is converted into a skating rink.

Another stamp that Nelson Rockefeller left indelibly upon the Empire State Plaza was his personal taste in art. The dream nursed by some early planners of the Capitol to make it a repository of fine art finally came true in the Plaza, though in a

Fireworks over the Empire State Plaza

Alexander Calder, *Triangles and Arches*

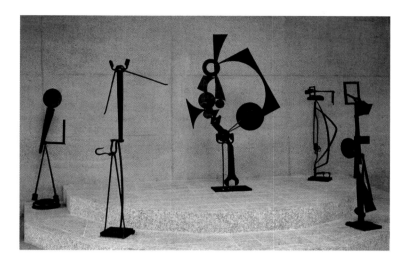

David Smith, *Voltri-Bolton Landing Series*

radically different idiom. Rockefeller thought of it as partly as a gallery of contemporary art. At the outset a sum of $2,653,000 was earmarked for works of art, both paintings and sculptures, to adorn the Plaza and its buildings. The governor, famed for his private art collections, appointed a commission of experts to select the works. As chairman of this commission he named Wallace Harrison, who saw eye to eye with him on modern abstract art. Rockefeller personally approved every piece before its purchase. The main criterion was that they be contemporary works by New York State artists, although there were exceptions. The choices were made during the 1960s. A total of 92 pieces were acquired at a cost of $1,887,610. Viewed simply as investments, apart from their aesthetic worth, they have appreciated greatly in value since their purchase. A New York art critic wrote of the collection: "Its quality is such that any museum in the western world specializing in contemporary art would be proud to have it."[22]

Forty of the paintings adorn the walls of the Concourse. The Concourse also presents, at intervals, a number of arresting metal sculptures. Even visitors who decry the bold abstractions must admit that representational works of art would have seemed out of place, and too small, for these expanses of wall. Nor would pictorial canvases blend with the architecture. One

Jason Seley, *Colleoni II*

does not find here the pompous portrait, the English hunting print, the soothing harbor scene, or a Grandma Moses primitive. In four instances, the paintings are of unusual length, and these were commissioned for the spaces they occupy. The longest, an untitled entry by Sven Lukin, stretches to 118 feet 7 inches.

Three sculptures on the plaza win particular notice. The most conspicuous, due to its location in the south reflecting pool silhouetted against the facade of the Cultural Education Center, is Alexander Calder's stabile, *Triangles and Arches.* A jagged cluster of black sheetmetal uprights, aiming sharpened spikes at the sky, makes a powerful impression from any angle. Fascinating to all visitors is George Rickey's *Two Lines Oblique,* a kinetic creation, whose elegantly tapered arms of stainless steel mounted on a forked post wave about in varied geometric attitudes, powered by the slightest breeze. The largest and costliest sculpture of the entire collection is an intricate wooden composition which spreads itself in the southeast corner of the Plaza.

Entitled *Labyrinth,* this was done on commission by a French sculptor, Francis Stahly. It is fashioned from iroko blocks and covers an area measuring 180 by 70 feet.

The Legislative Office Building was hastened to early completion to mollify grumbling legislators impatient to escape their crowded Capitol nooks. They began moving into their spacious office suites in January 1972. This building, too, was favored with its modest share of art, but with a difference. A minor revolt against the Rockefeller taste occurred among some lawmakers who disliked modern art. Accordingly, the Legislature set up its own committee to select pieces, which were to be "strictly representational."

The Empire State Plaza was destined for more ceremonies of a dedicatory nature. A much-publicized celebration, tied in with the U.S. Bicentennial, took place on July 1, 1976. This observance marked the opening of the Cultural Education Center along with the new State Museum, but it signalized the

Empire State Plaza Art Collection at Corning Tower

Education Center by snipping a ribbon crossing the doors at the Terrace level. Crowds trooped through the Adirondack Hall, first completed wing of the State Museum.

On Memorial Day 1978 another ribbon-cutting ceremony was held for The Egg—the Performing Arts Center—which signified not only the completion of that structure but of the Mall project in its entirety. With that occasion, John C. Byron retired, amid plaudits, from his crowning career as director of construction. Within a few days, Nelson A. Rockefeller observed his 70th birthday.

In May 1978 the AFL-CIO of New York State launched a movement asking the Legislature to rename the Mall as the Governor Nelson A. Rockefeller Empire State Plaza. The Senate quickly and overwhelmingly passed a resolution endorsing that request, and a bill was introduced to that effect. The bill died a quiet death in the Democrat-controlled Assembly. Ignoring the legislative inaction, Governor Carey issued an Executive Order declaring that the Plaza "shall henceforth be known as The Governor Nelson A. Rockefeller Empire State Plaza."

By now "out of politics" and a private citizen, Nelson Rockefeller made his farewell appearance at his beloved Plaza on

Francois Stahly, *Labyrinth*

public debut of the Plaza as a whole. Governor Hugh L. Carey led a retinue of state officials to the platform and pronounced the Plaza "a monument to the people."[23] A band played and toy balloons ascended. As a climax, the Chancellor of the Board of Regents, Theodore M. Black, officially opened the Cultural

Empire State Plaza, looking west

October 6, 1978, to accept that honor. He was accompanied by his wife Happy and several other members of the Rockefeller family. A considerable audience assembled around the granite monument he had previously placed there for dedication of the Empire State Plaza, They heard Governor Carey intone, "Today we are gathered at the most beautiful state capital in America, to honor one of America's most civic-minded citizens. . . . What was constructed was more than buildings. This complex is a unique concentration of great architecture, great art, and of New York's place in history. . . . A deteriorated capital city could not, and cannot, be accepted as part of New York State's legacy."

In his acceptance remarks, Rockefeller praised Governor Carey as "a man with courage and humanity to stop long enough and recognize the efforts of a former governor before he is dead."

Aerial view of the Capitol building and the Empire State Plaza

On January 26, 1979, Nelson A. Rockefeller died of a heart attack in New York City.

The great Plaza bearing his name became an enduring symbol of Rockefeller's governorship. It bloomed into a civic, convention, entertainment, and cultural center, as well as a magnetic tourist and visitor attraction. Long before its completion, its impact on the surrounding community became obvious. Neigh-borhood improvement groups sprang up around its periphery: the Center Square Neighborhood Association expanded its prior efforts; others were organized—Hudson Park, the Washington Avenue Association, Robinson Square, and the Mansion Neighborhood Association. In response to the demolition of countless structures, Historic Albany Foundation was organized in 1974 to protect and preserve the city's historic buildings.

Capitol and Empire State Plaza

Assembly Staircase, restored laylight

CHAPTER FIFTEEN

RESTORATION OF THE CAPITOL, 1977–2013

DIANA S. WAITE

South facade

THE NEW YORK STATE CAPITOL SITS MAJESTICALLY AT THE HEAD OF ALBANY'S State Street, a masterpiece of civic architecture with superlatively executed interior features and finishes. The restoration work undertaken since 1977 is a tribute to the perseverance of its four original architects—Thomas Fuller, Leopold Eidlitz, Henry Hobson Richardson, and Isaac Perry—who labored under geologically difficult, structurally challenging, and politically exasperating conditions. The restoration work also salutes the hundreds of highly skilled masons, exceptional stone carvers, and other craftspeople who built the Capitol.

The completion of the restoration and rehabilitation work will help ensure that the many people who today occupy and visit the building—young and old, New Yorkers and visitors, the disabled and the able bodied—will be able to do so safely and at the same time be inspired by the values that it represents. Completing the work will help sustain an educated constituency for the Capitol—new generations who will be better able to understand the building and be prepared to continue to preserve it in the years to come.

The Temporary State Commission on the Capitol and the 1982 Master Plan

The restoration of the New York State Capitol has its roots in the late 1970s, when the restoration of the Senate Chamber was underway. That project set such a dazzling example and sterling standard that it prompted the Senate and the Assembly to pass legislation creating a Temporary State Commission on the Restoration of the Capitol.[1]

The legislation also detailed the current condition of the building. Over the years, in an attempt to provide more office space for state government, major sections of the Capitol had been subjected to "scores of piecemeal structural changes designed in haste and without the benefit of a central theme." The outcomes had proved entirely unsatisfactory: "the beauty of the original interior," the bill explained, had been "marred,

Temporary State Commission on the Restoration of the Capitol, left to right: Lewis A. Swyer, Norman S. Rice, Frank E. Sanchis III, Stuart W. Stein, Barnabas McHenry, Steven L. Einhorn, Orin Lehman, Matthew Bender IV, Patrick Bulgaro, James O'Shea, 1979

hidden or subdivided by partition in a style befitting neither the utility nor the grandeur of the building." The task before the new Temporary State Commission on the Restoration of the Capitol would be "to make a complete study and recommend a master plan for the long term restoration and renovation" of the building. There would be eleven commissioners—three appointed by the governor, six by the Senate and Assembly, plus the Commissioner of the Office of General Services and the Commissioner of the Office of Parks and Recreation.[2]

Governor Hugh L. Carey signed the bill into law in 1979. The commission began its work that same year and issued a 152-page master plan in December 1982. The master plan endorsed the excellent restoration of the Senate Chamber and recommended that "this same degree of historical accuracy and artistic distinction" be "integrated with the overall plan for the building's restoration and rehabilitation."[3] Work on the master plan began with the preparation of a historic structure report—a comprehensive study of the original design and construction of the building and an analysis of its current physical condition.[4] The historic structure report and the master plan were intended to provide commission members with a basis for making comprehensive recommendations about the building's future based on firm documentation, rather than on conjecture or personal tastes.[5]

The recommendations put forth in the master plan were comprehensive and ambitious. They dealt with restoring significant historic spaces and spatial relationships in the building and improving its functionality and safety as a contemporary seat of government. Some spaces should be restored, the plan stated, while others should be rehabilitated or reconstructed; some areas would require new construction, and all would need continual, careful maintenance.[6] Many of the major recommendations in the master plan have been accomplished during the past three decades, with splendid results. However, several significant recommendations from the master plan still await funding and implementation.

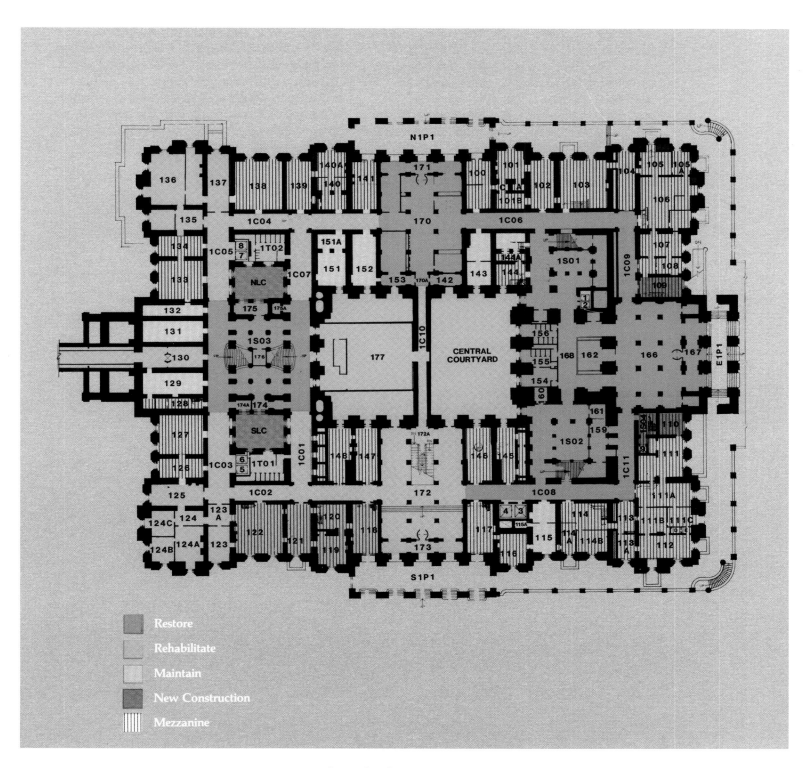

First floor plan from 1982 master plan

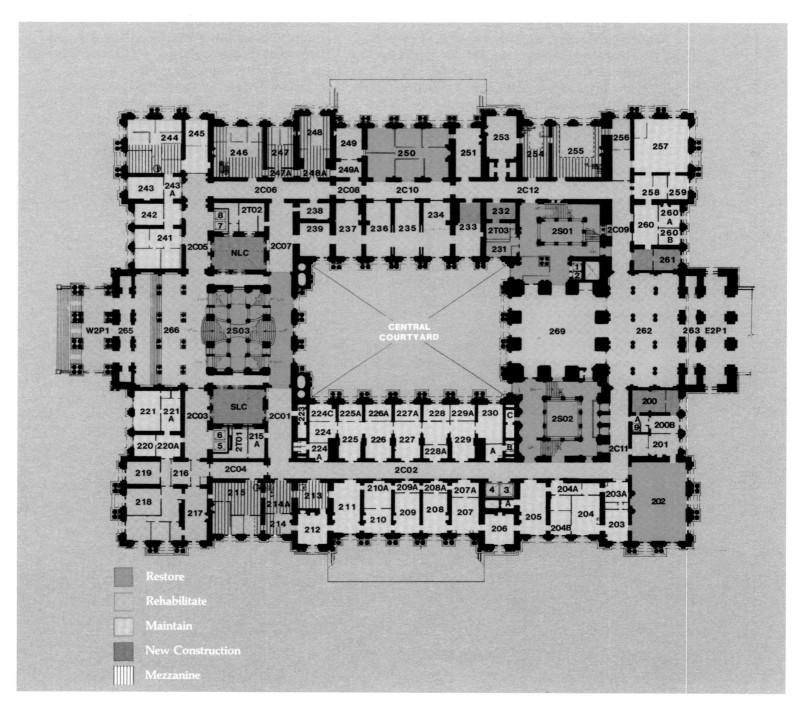

Second floor plan from 1982 master plan

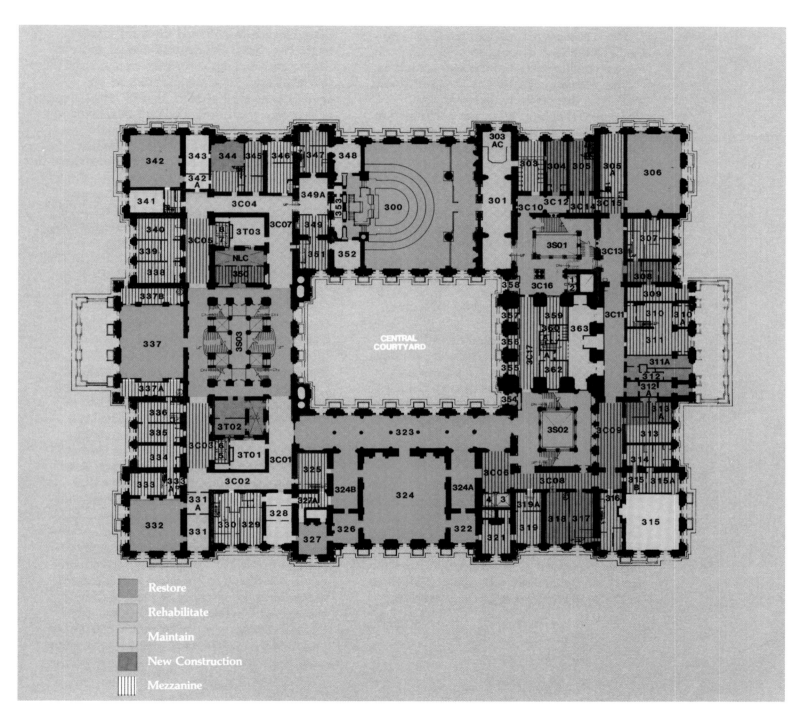

Third floor plan from 1982 master plan

Senate Chamber

Senate Chamber and Lobbies (Room 324, Rooms 324A and B, Room 323, Room 425, Room 4C08)

Of the many spaces in the Capitol designed by Henry Hobson Richardson, the Senate Chamber was the most richly decorated and monumental. Its restoration began in 1977, under Senate Majority Leader Warren M. Anderson and with the commitment of Roger C. Thompson, the Secretary of the Senate, who was dissatisfied with the condition of the Senate Chamber and its associated spaces. Thompson had overseen the badly needed cleaning of the stone in the third floor Senate lobby and realized that other problems needed to be corrected immediately—the overloaded electrical system, inadequate air conditioning, threadbare carpeting, and inappropriate chandeliers. He called on the firm of Mendel Mesick Cohen Waite Architects later that year. John I. Mesick, the partner in charge for the project, remembered an exasperated Thompson remarking, "This lobby does not possess a sense of history—the place appears little better than a third rate hotel! What should be done?"[7]

Over the next few years the Senate pushed through a program to restore not just its lobby but also its corridors and the Chamber itself. The work began with the preparation of a historic structure report, which included an illustrated history of the Chamber and measured drawings and detailed descriptions of the existing conditions. When the Chamber was opened in 1881, there were just 32 senators. By 1977 there were 60, and the additional desks had squeezed out seats for aides along the walls. A staff office had been built into a corner of the Chamber, and security glazing had been installed at the front of the visitors' galleries during the turbulent 1960s.

The restoration work began in June 1978 after the close of the legislative session, based on the recommendations of consulting preservation architects. Many of the later accretions were removed from the Chamber and lobbies, not only reinstating the original architectural design but also relieving congestion and improving circulation. The stone walls were cleaned; the stained glass repaired, and the gilded leather wall covering replicated

Senate Chamber

in fiberglass. Reproduction brass chandeliers and sconces were hung, and the original carpeting reproduced. The Senate desk was reconfigured to its original design and size. The senators' desks were arranged in tighter concentric circles, and the settees along the walls reinstated. More work was needed, but the Chamber was ready when the Senate reconvened in January 1979.

Over the next three years, monumental gates of mild steel, bronze, and brass were hung to separate the public corridor from the Senate lobbies, where senators could confer privately. Original furniture was reproduced. New decorative glass was installed in the windows in the north wall of the corridor.[8] Later, encaustic tile was installed in the third floor corridor. Work on the Senate elevator lobby was completed in 2009.

Senate corridor, fourth floor

Senate lobby gates

Executive Chamber, fireplace

Executive Chamber (Room 202)

The Executive Chamber, completed in 1881 and long known as the Red Room, was initially used by Governors Alonzo B. Cornell and Grover Cleveland as their working offices. Subsequent governors have used adjoining smaller spaces as their offices and utilized the Executive Chamber as a ceremonial space. It has also served as a reception room and for cabinet meetings and press conferences.

The Executive Chamber is one of architect H. H. Richardson's most important rooms in the Capitol.[9] His design included the coffered ceiling and walls enriched with mahogany wainscoting and gilded leather. The tall arched windows were framed with polished marble. Richardson also designed the furnishings.

The restoration of the Executive Chamber was the first major project to be completed in response to the master plan for the Capitol.[10] Carried out under the direction of the Office of General Services and the Capitol Architect in 1984–85, the project returned the room to its appearance in 1881 and now provides an impressive setting for official gubernatorial events. The marble and woodwork were cleaned, and the carpeting and wall covering reproduced. A polished brass gasolier and sconces like those in the Senate Chamber were hung. The heating and

Executive Chamber, looking east

Executive Chamber, stained-glass transoms

Executive Chamber, embroidered draperies

Senate Conference Rooms

Senate Conference Room, fireplace

air-conditioning units under the windows were removed, and the HVAC system replaced. The windows were restored to their full height, and the lunettes filled with stained glass.[11] The restored Executive Chamber was rededicated on May 13, 1985, by Governor Mario M. Cuomo.

Senate Conference Rooms (Rooms 123, 124, 125)

These three Senate conference rooms, located at the southwest corner of the Capitol, were once used as office suites. Designed by architect Isaac Perry and completed in 1896, they have massive stone fireplaces and high ceilings. In 1912, Room 124 was divided into smaller rooms, and oak wainscoting was installed, probably in response to water damage from the 1911 fire.

Leopold Eidlitz's Court of Appeals

In 1981 the Temporary State Commission on the Restoration of the Capitol recommended that these rooms "be preserved in their original architectural configuration, including finishes, for the future."[12] Within a few months architectural drawings had been prepared for the rehabilitation of the rooms, which included removal of the partitions in Room 124.[13] The rooms were restored to their ca. 1896 appearance between 1983 and 1987.[14]

Former Court of Appeals (Room 250)

Architect Leopold Eidlitz allocated this space on the second floor for the Court of Appeals, the state's highest court, and construction was completed in 1879. The court, however, used the space only briefly, until 1884, when it moved to Room 315, a new courtroom designed by H. H. Richardson (Room 315's appointments were moved in 1917 to the Court of Appeals building on Eagle Street).[15]

In 1889–90, after the Golden Corridor was removed because of structural problems, Room 250 was reconfigured by architect Isaac Perry, but he retained many of the important elements of Eidlitz's design, including the coffered oak ceiling and carved paneling. Perry moved the south wall farther to the north, reducing the size of the room by nearly half; the remaining space became an east-west corridor. The stone chimneypiece was shifted to the center of the east wall, and new stone trim added.[16] During the mid-twentieth century, when the room was converted to offices, it was filled with partitions and suspended fluorescent lights.

The 1982 master plan called for the space to be restored to Perry's design and used for hearings and conferences. However, as more of Eidlitz's original design was rediscovered, a 1984 consultant's report recommended "reinstating the pre-1890 decorative program by replicating the Eidlitz carpet, drapes and polychromatic paint scheme in the upper wall areas," along with chandeliers and sconces of that era.[17] However, rather than its other features being restored, this room, which is also known as the Blue Room, was reconfigured in 1983 as a temporary pressroom for the governor's press conferences. The television lighting systems were left exposed in order to minimize danger to the historic fabric of the room.[18]

Governor's Reception Room (Room 269)

Beginning with its first architect, Thomas Fuller, the designs for the Capitol had included a spectacular ten-story tower rising above the east facade. However, its construction was eventually abandoned after engineers decided that the hill's clayey soil could not support the tower's weight. Meanwhile, though, the base for the tower had been constructed as far as the fifth floor, creating within its walls an open, multistory rotunda. By 1900 new floors had been inserted in the rotunda. Room 269, at the second story level, was intended to be part of a sequence of ceremonial spaces leading from the Eastern Approach staircase and connecting the East Lobby and the Assembly and Senate staircases with the Hall of Governors and the Executive Chamber.[19]

Two decades later, a new plan called for the floor of Room 269 to be removed, thereby creating a two story, 40 foot tall space to be used as a Hall of Flags. William deLeftwich Dodge, a prominent muralist, was engaged to create allegorical paintings of the military history of New York State for the ceiling. He painted most of the murals on canvas in his Manhattan studio and installed them in the Capitol in 1929. The Goddess of Har-

Room 269, ca. 1960

Room 269, Governor's Reception Room, after restoration

mony, or Spirit of New York, is surrounded by panels depicting the Five Nations of the Iroquois and the major cultural groups that settled the state, as well as important land and naval battles and military leaders. However, with the onset of the Great Depression, the floor of the room was never removed, and the murals thus have never been seen as the artist anticipated. During World War II, wood and glass partitions were installed to create small offices, and in 1969 the room was remodeled as a conference space. In the 1980s it was again subdivided into offices.

The 1982 master plan called for Room 269 to be used as a Hall of Military Record for displaying collections of the State Division of Military and Naval Affairs, but the project stalled.[20] In response to inquiries from the governor's staff, the State Commission on the Restoration of the Capitol presented a series of proposals for reuse of the room and guidelines for the restoration of the Dodge murals. Finally, in 1993 Governor Mario M. Cuomo, after consulting the State Commission on the Restoration of the Capitol, decided that the room should become a ceremonial space.[21]

The murals were restored, and the marble paving was repaired. The granite walls were cleaned, and double-leaf oak doors were reproduced for the east opening. Custom bronze torchères were fabricated to illuminate the mural and the room. Because of budget limitations, the windows were repaired rather than restored. In January 1997, Governor George E. Pataki dedicated the room as the Governor's Reception Room. It is used as a waiting room for people visiting the governor and his staff, and is open to the public.

Assembly Chamber and Lobbies (Rooms 300, 301, 349, 349A)

Designed by Leopold Eidlitz and completed in 1879, the Assembly Chamber was acclaimed as the "most monumental interior in America" and as one of the most architecturally distinctive spaces in the country. The soaring sandstone ceiling was said to be the widest vaulted span constructed anywhere in the world.[22]

Constructed of granite, marble, and sandstone of four different colors, the Assembly Chamber filled nearly all of the

Assembly Chamber, 1879

north part of the third floor. The sandstone walls and ceiling were incised with stylized floral designs and enriched with red, ultramarine, black, and metallic gold pigments. The room was illuminated by sixteen monumental floor-mounted bronze gasoliers, rather than by hanging fixtures. The furniture was solid mahogany upholstered in red leather. Artist William Morris Hunt created two luminous, allegorical murals above the windows on the north and south walls, *The Flight of Night* and *The Discoverer*.

The Assembly Chamber, however, was soon plagued with acoustical problems, and the overstressed stone vaults began to fail almost immediately.[23] The vaulting was finally replaced with steel trusses in 1889, and a lower, coffered ceiling of oak and papier-mâché was substituted.[24] New lighting was installed. Hunt's murals, by then disintegrating from seeping moisture, were hidden above the new ceiling.[25]

Over the years, other modifications were made to the Assembly Chamber. The areas behind the visitors' galleries were filled in. The rostrum was reconfigured several times, and the members' chairs and desks were replaced. Sections of the sandstone walls were covered with cork tiles in an attempt to improve acoustics. A room was partitioned off at the north end of the east lobby. Under Governor Nelson A. Rockefeller, the feasibility of restoring Eidlitz's vaulted ceiling was explored, but no further action was taken.

The 1982 master plan proposed that the Assembly Chamber be returned to its 1889 form. Five years later Assembly Speaker Melvin Miller requested that the Commission on the Restoration of the Capitol prepare a preliminary project statement for restoration work. That report led to an architectural study that recommended reconstructing Eidlitz's 1879 vaulted ceiling, reinstating the original decorative scheme, installing up-to-date mechanical and information systems, and restoring the Assembly lobbies and adjoining offices.[26] A fiscal crisis largely contributed to postponing this work.

Between 1998 and 2002, ramps were built at the east entrance vestibule, in the west lobby and corridor, beside the rostrum, and in the visitors' galleries, in order to make the Chamber accessible to the disabled. Reproduction doors at the east vestibule were installed, along with carpeting in the Chamber. Blocked archways in the visitors' galleries were restored and new seating put in place.[27]

In 2002, the Assembly, under Speaker Sheldon Silver, requested proposals from architects to restore the Chamber and update the mechanical systems. A master plan was prepared, and architects and engineers began studies for restoring the ceiling

Assembly Chamber, demolishing infill masonry

Assembly Chamber, restoring the galleries

Assembly Chamber, restored gallery vault

Assembly Chamber, looking west

Assembly Chamber, restored
stained-glass windows
and decorative painting

Assembly Chamber, east entrance
ramp and stair

Assembly Chamber, East Lobby with
restored Minton encaustic tile floor

Assembly Chamber, restored lamp
standards in the East Lobby

to its 1879 appearance. As a first step, the existing wrought-iron trusses were reinforced to carry the weight of a fifth floor mezzanine housing more efficient HVAC equipment. The electrical system was replaced, and the fire protection system was modified to meet modern code requirements. Studies were undertaken to show how reproduction vaults made of a composite material could be hung from new steel trusses in the attic, rather than requiring support from the original columns. In addition, the east lobby was restored to its 1879 design, including replicas of Eidlitz's torchères and reproduction encaustic and geometric tile flooring. The original decorative paint scheme was reinstated to the walls of the Chamber, and the stained glass windows were conserved.[28] The work in the Chamber was initiated and funded by the Assembly.

Assembly Speaker's Conference Room

Speaker of the Assembly's Conference Room (Room 342)

Before the 1911 fire, this area housed a portion of the State Library, with Room 342 being a reading room. After the fire, this area was redesigned in the Beaux-Arts style, initially by state architect Franklin Ware and then by his successor, Lewis Pilcher. Room 342 became a legislative committee room.

Over the years, Room 342 had remained largely intact, including the mantelpiece and overmantel made of Siena marble, and the elaborate plaster ceiling with coffers and rosettes. However, adjustments had been made to accommodate radiators; and the window lunettes had been covered over. The original chandeliers were replaced around 1950. The 1982 master plan called for the restoration of the room's Beaux-Arts features.[29]

Rehabilitation and restoration of the conference room was begun in 2002 and completed the next year.[30] The quartered-oak paneling was cleaned, and the faux Caen stone above the paneling was restored. New windows were installed to match the height of the originals.

Speaker of the Assembly's Suite (Rooms 351 and 352)

A new reception and private meeting room for the Speaker of the Assembly (Room 351) was created in 2002–03 in an area adjacent to the Speaker's Office; this work involved removing a mezzanine and the 1940s wall systems, reinstating the windows to their full height, and adding new glass walls and lighting.[31]

Room 352, the Speaker's Office, which had been obscured by partitions and dropped ceilings, was returned to its original proportions in 2006–07. The stonework was cleaned, the fireplace restored, and the lighting fixtures and original doors and hardware replicated. Later, Leopold Eidlitz's paint scheme was reproduced on the ceiling and carved stone trim.[32]

Assembly Speaker's Office   Assembly Speaker's Office

completed about 1880. The room was furnished with cast-brass gas and electric sconces and chandeliers, and the upper sections of the carmine-painted walls were stenciled with a polychrome pattern of white, blue, and gold. Room 305A, the space adjacent to the west wall of the Parlor, originally served as a lobby.[35]

Over the years, the parlor was altered. A bronze bas-relief of *Hudson Trading with the Manhattoes,* by John Francis Brines, was positioned over the fireplace, and an ornate bronze panel placed in the hearth. Between 1949 and 1951, the original lighting fixtures were removed, and doorways on the south and west walls were closed up. Oak wainscoting was installed, and stenciled plaster panels were added above the wainscoting. The original windows were taken out, and the bead-boarded recessed panels in the coffered ceiling were removed.[36]

Assembly Majority Leader's Office (Rooms 340 and 341)

These two rooms were originally part of the State Library. After the 1911 fire, Room 341 was redesigned to accommodate the Assembly Ways and Means Committee, with an entryway, antechamber, and restroom. The walls were covered with oak paneling and rough plaster above. The ceiling was enriched with plaster vines and interlocking squares.

Both rooms were renovated in the 1940s. Room 341 was subdivided to provide a separate space for secretaries, and a mezzanine and stairway were added.[33] In a recent renovation the partition was lowered, and a glass ceiling inserted over the smaller space.[34]

Assembly Parlor (Room 306)

The Assembly Parlor was designed by Leopold Eidlitz, the architect of the Assembly Chamber, and was intended for use by Assembly members when meeting with constituents. It was

Assembly Parlor, fireplace and restored sconces

Assembly Parlor

The master plan recommended restoring the Assembly Parlor to its original appearance and furnishing it with reproductions of the original carpeting, wall treatments, and lighting fixtures. Funded by the Assembly, work began in 2002 and was completed the next year. The lunette transoms over the windows were uncovered, and new central-pivot windows were installed, reinstating them nearly to their full height. The wainscoting, baseboards, and plaster panels were removed; the walls were then plastered, and the upper sections were stenciled.[37]

Great Western Staircase (Room S03)

The Great Western Staircase, nicknamed the Million Dollar Staircase because of its cost, takes up nearly one-third of the west side of the Capitol, rising nearly 120 feet to the laylight. Inspired by Charles Garnier's grand lobby of the Paris Opera House, H. H. Richardson designed this space as an elegant composition of arches and vaults surmounted by a dome and oculus. Construction began in 1883, using primarily Corsehill red sandstone from Scotland, limestone from Indiana, and granite from New England and New Brunswick. Medina sandstone from western New York was used for the stair treads.[38]

After Richardson's death in 1886, architect Isaac Perry substituted a gabled skylight for the dome and added a skylight and arched laylight. Perry worked closely with Louis Hinton, the foreman who supervised the 500 stone carvers executing the botanical compositions, historical scenes, and portraits of American men, women, and children for which the staircase is famously known. The electric lighting system was then among the largest in any U.S. public building.

The 1911 fire that consumed the State Library melted some of the stonework on the staircase and destroyed the skylight and laylight. The replacement skylight was removed in 1968, thereby cutting off an important source of natural light.

The master plan recommended that the staircase be restored to its appearance following the repairs made after the fire, in order to "improve safety, enhance public appreciation and clarify orientation" for legislators and visitors alike. The stonework was to be cleaned; the skylight and laylight rebuilt; and the lighting fixtures repaired.

In 2001 experts analyzed the stone and the soiling. Beginning in 2006, the staircase and the west entrance lobby were cleaned using a latex product infused with detergent; it was sprayed on and then peeled away, removing the grime. The c. 1912 cast-bronze lighting fixtures on the staircase were cleaned,

Great Western Staircase, laylight before restoration

Great Western Staircase, after cleaning

Great Western Staircase, glass being installed
in slope of main skylight and side corridor

repaired, repatinated, and rewired; other nearby fixtures were also cleaned. A storage area under the stairs was removed and the corridor restored to its original design. The total project cost was $2.8 million.[39]

Meanwhile, in 2000, work had begun on the skylight, which filled both sloping sides of the gabled roof above the stairs. The work was carried out under the direction of the Office of General Services.[40] Replicating the original skylight was explored but set aside because of insufficient documentation and reservations about leakage and thermal performance of the original design. For those reasons and because the skylight would not be visu-

ally prominent, the skylight was rebuilt using modern materials, including insulated glass units and extruded-aluminum rafters placed on top of the existing steel trusses.

Although the steel framing and textured-wire glazing survived from the 1912 laylight, many components had been altered or damaged. Wallpaper had been glued onto the glass and painted gold. Many of the panes were broken or badly scratched or had been replaced with sheet metal. For those reasons and because of safety concerns, OGS decided to replicate the glazing by laminating a PVB layer in between two layers of annealed textured glass. The frame of the laylight was painted

Restored Great Western Staircase

a light green to match an earlier coating. Artificial lighting was installed behind the diffuser to supplement the natural light.

Roof Projects

Designed by H. H. Richardson and Leopold Eidlitz, the original roofs were supported by iron and steel trusses resting on the masonry bearing walls. The main roofs were covered with dark blue slate from Pennsylvania. Barrel tiles, made of red-orange terra cotta, outlined the corners of the towers and the hips of the main roofs. Monumental terra cotta finials, 28 feet tall, marked the apexes of the tower roofs, and flat terra cotta tiles covered their surfaces.[41]

Over the years, as state government expanded, roof ridges were raised, and dormers were inserted to accommodate additional offices, altering the profiles of the roof. The skylights over the Senate and Assembly staircases were covered over during the 1940s, and the skylight over the Great Western Staircase was removed in 1968.[42] Much of the roofing was replaced with black slate from Wales in 1968. The corner towers were reroofed with flat orange terra cotta shingled tiles, but the other terra cotta elements were retained.[43]

The 1982 master plan recommended that the overall profile of the roof and the slate coverings be maintained and that the three major skylights be reconstructed.

An engineering report commissioned by the Office of General Services in 1996 found that while the roof appeared from street level to be in good condition, deferred maintenance had created serious problems. Water leaks were causing damage to interior finishes and exterior walls. The Capitol needed to undergo an "aggressive program of roof replacement and

Great Western Staircase

repairs" that would use traditional materials in order to maintain its historic appearance.[44]

The roofing work was executed in four phases. Phase one, on the west facade, began in 2000 and was completed in 2004. It included replacing the monumental terra cotta components and installing new flashing and waterproofing systems, as well as the work on the skylight and laylight over the Great Western Staircase. Replacing terra cotta elements, installing flashing and waterproofing systems, and repointing dormers and chimneys were undertaken on the north quadrant of the roof during phase two (2002–06) and phase three (begun 2005), which addressed the south quadrant.[45] Balusters at the base of the slate roofs were reconstructed.[46] In 2008 the massive granite coping stones on the west gable were removed, new flashing installed, and the stones put back in place.[47] Much of the Capitol was surrounded by scaffolding from 2000 through the completion of phase four in October 2012.

Phase four, on the east quadrant of the building, required relocating tenants and conducting the work in a crowded, occupied building while retaining access for state officials and visitors. The skylights and laylights over both the Assembly and the Senate staircases were reinstated. A new roof, 15 feet higher than the original, was constructed over Tower Hall, and a mezzanine was suspended from the roof beams to create more office space. New flagpoles were added. Inside the building, the north corridor was reconfigured, and restrooms and a new staircase between the fourth and fifth floors added. The fifth floor level of the Senate Staircase and Tower Hall were cleaned. In addition, the balcony above the Assembly Staircase at the fourth floor mezzanine was reconstructed, and the original decorative painting scheme on the fifth floor restored.[48] The total cost of

East facade, with scaffolding and crane

Rehabilitation of east central roof

East central roof, overlooking Empire State Plaza to the south

Terra-cotta finial removed for replication

Staging and access for the northeast tower

tance. He engaged Peter Lehrer, a noted construction expert, to provide pro bono insight and recommendations. As a result, the workforce was doubled; the number of shifts increased; and the schedule was adjusted so that the different trades could work simultaneously instead of sequentially. The available work areas for the contractors were also increased. These actions resulted in the construction work being completed two years ahead of schedule and with a savings of $2.8 million.

Removing slate shingles and terra-cotta hip rolls

phase four was $49 million, making the total of the fourteen years of work $74.6 million.[49]

Work on phase four had begun in the summer of 2009. In January 2011, soon after taking office, Governor Andrew M. Cuomo announced a new plan that would accelerate the timetable and save money. The revised work plan was part of a larger effort initiated by Governor Cuomo to make the Capitol more accessible to visitors and highlight the building's historic impor-

Assembly and Senate Staircases (Rooms S01, S02)

The Assembly Staircase, located in the northeast quadrant of the Capitol, rises a full four stories, connecting the first floor lobbies and corridors with the Executive Offices on the second floor and the Assembly Chamber and galleries on the third and fourth floors. Similarly, the Senate Staircase, located in the southeast quadrant, provides access to the second floor and

Left: Assembly Staircase, ca. 1880. Right: Assembly Staircase, showing laylight, wall stencils, and balcony (the image was reversed in an 1882 publication)

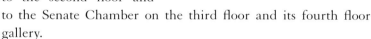

In 1885, architect Isaac Perry cut round-arched openings in the walls to admit more light. In 1888, cracks began to open in the lower parts of the staircase and engineers proposed that it be rebuilt. However, corrective work did not begin until 1906, when the first floor columns and piers were replaced. When the fifth story was added in 1949, the sandstone balcony and parts of the belt courses were torn out.[53] The windows were filled in, and new lighting fixtures hung.[54]

to the Senate Chamber on the third floor and its fourth floor gallery.

Architect Thomas Fuller's scheme for the Assembly Staircase, which incorporated many iron elements, was roundly criticized for being "faulty in construction."[50] Leopold Eidlitz, the architect of the Assembly Chamber, created a new design for the staircase, keeping Fuller's overall dimensions and east-west axis but using sandstone throughout. Eidlitz's design had pointed arches and stone piers in the stairwell and railings pierced with quatrefoils. Construction began in 1877 and was completed in 1879.

The walls, originally painted a dark maroon, were soon repainted a "warm red-brown" enriched with a "band of gold, marked with a conventional floral pattern in vermillion" about four feet above the treads and floors. Archways and doors were picked out in gold. The fourth floor walls were stenciled with red and gold diaper designs. The sandstone cornice was enriched with ultramarine and vermilion pigments, much like the color scheme used in the Assembly Chamber.[51] A laylight originally filled the entire ceiling area. Sconces and gasoliers with frosted-glass globes filtered the gaslight.[52]

Like the Assembly Staircase, the Senate Staircase was designed by Leopold Eidlitz and modified by Isaac Perry. Constructed of Corsehill red sandstone and granite beginning in 1883, it features richly carved flying buttresses, a monumental "rose window" of carved stone, and bas-reliefs of animals. A plate-glass skylight was installed in 1885, but the laylight, to be made of opalescent glass, was not put in place until 1896.[55] Over time, the character of the space was eroded as arched openings were closed, a fifth story inserted, and midcentury lighting fixtures installed.[56] During World War II the skylights over both staircases were scheduled for "blackout painting," in order to avoid aiding enemy planes.

The master plan recommended that both staircases and their skylights be restored, in order to improve public safety through better illumination of the stairs themselves.[57]

Work on the Assembly Staircase began in 1997 with the restoration of the early decorative scheme on the third and fourth story walls. The sandstone was cleaned in 1998 and the decorative elements reinstated on the first through fourth floors.[58] A few years later, as part of phase four of the roof rehabilitation, the Office of General Services began exploring the feasibility of restoring the skylights over both staircases.[59]

Assembly Staircase, underside of fifth-floor infill

Assembly Staircase, recreation of stencil patterns

Restoring the upper levels of the Assembly Staircase required removal of the fifth story. The surviving sections of the original cornice were cleaned and then replicated where it was missing on the other walls, using sandstone from the Wallace quarries in Nova Scotia. Based on historic paint investigations, the upper sections of the staircase wall were decorated with Moorish diaper and floral patterns. The balustrade and brackets of the balcony on the west wall, which had been removed when the fifth story was added, were recreated using 3-D computer models and then carved in sandstone, starting with computer-guided drills and then finishing the work by hand.[60]

Despite extensive research, little documentation about the design or materials of the Assembly laylight was uncovered: only one image, an 1882 rendering, was located, and only a few pieces of physical evidence survived—fragments of broken glass and traces of the structure that held the laylight in place. The Commission on the Restoration of the Capitol endorsed a design approach that included new interpretations of the state's fauna and flora, which were painted by German artisans onto hand-blown panels of colored glass. The clear glass panels to either side were sandblasted with patterns.

The skylight over the laylight was assembled using clear, heat-strengthened insulated glass on the exterior and clear laminated safety glass on the interior. The glass was set in new steel framing suspended from the original steel trusses. Fixtures with fluorescent bulbs between the skylight and laylight supplement the natural light and provide emergency lighting.

Restoration of the Senate Staircase and its laylight similarly involved the removal of the fifth story. Stone finishes at the top of the staircase were restored, and the original windows openings reestablished. No evidence of the original appearance of the laylight had survived. Two later drawings supplied some details about the framing, and a few fragments of glass from the skylight provided a few clues about its finish and color.[61] The Commission on the Restoration of the Capitol again endorsed a separate design approach for the laylight; since there was no evidence of the original, the new one would

Assembly Staircase, restored decorative scheme

Assembly Staircase, reconstructed skylight

Assembly Staircase, painted and etched glass in the laylight

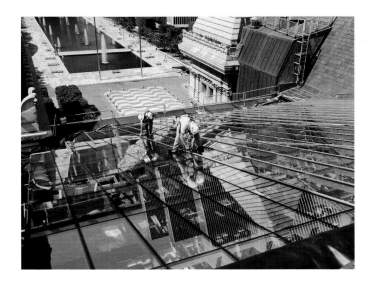

Senate Staircase, skylight

2009. The Assembly laylight was completed in December 2011 and officially unveiled to the public on January 4, 2012, as part of Governor Andrew M. Cuomo's State of the State ceremonies. Almost exactly a year later, on January 9, 2013, the Senate laylight was unveiled by Governor Cuomo, again as part of his State of the State ceremonies.[64]

Senate Staircase, mock-up of opalescent, slumped, and stained-glass panels in the laylight

Senate Staircase, restored laylight

follow the historic framing systems.[62] The final design incorporated a three-part border and a field of cream-colored opalescent glass.[63]

Bids for reconstructing the laylights and skylights were received in 2008, and the construction contract was awarded in

Elevators

Elevators were part of the proposed circulation system for the Capitol from the outset. In 1879, four hydraulic elevators, two adjacent to the Assembly Staircase and two near the northwest light court, were put into service; they ran to the fourth floor. The two Senate elevators, also hydraulic, were installed in 1881; in 1905 they were extended to the fifth floor. The original machinery was retained, but new bronze doors and gates were added.[65]

Alterations to these six elevators, begun after the fire of 1911, were completed the next year. The hydraulic mechanisms were replaced with geared systems, and the Assembly elevators were extended to the fifth floor. Two new shafts, each accommodating two geared elevators, were constructed near the light courts.[66] Between 1948 and 1952 the hoistway doors and surrounds were largely remodeled on the upper floors.

The 1982 master plan for the Capitol reported that the existing elevators ran slowly but generally handled traffic adequately. The plan recommended that the elevators be converted from manual to automatic service to improve speed and safety and that the hoistways be enclosed in order to meet building codes.[67] However, those changes were not made, and the elevators continued to deteriorate, causing shutdowns, entrapment of passengers, and small fires.[68]

An engineering study carried out in 1997–98 addressed all eight elevators, but initially improvements were made only to the four on the west side of the building.[69] This phase included installing new hoisting equipment, motor controllers, and digital controls and replacing the manually operated scissor gates with automatic cab doors. The interiors of the new cabs were finished with brass panels and moldings. The new cab doors have fixed scissor gates of brass sandwiched between two sheets of glass. The historic wrought-iron hoistway gates were replaced with aluminum replicas.[70]

The Assembly and Senate elevators on the east side were not upgraded until phase two, carried out in 2004–09. These mechanical upgrades were similar to those of phase one. The

Aluminum hoistway doors, which replicated the original wrought-iron panels

Recreated Senate Chamber elevator entranceway

original brass scissor gates attached to the cabs were replaced with automatic sliding doors having cast-glass panels suggesting the appearance of the original gates. All of the upgraded elevators are fully automatic and meet ADA compliance requirements.

On the third floor, the 1950s marble hoistway doors and surrounds of two elevators were replaced with replicas of the original bronze doors and arched entranceways on the first and second floors. Marble wainscoting and moldings, sandstone baseboard and corner trim, and encaustic tile flooring were reconstructed.[71]

Hall of Governors and Hall of New York
(Rooms 2C01, 2C02, 2C11 and Rooms 2C08, SC09, 2C10, 2C12)

The portrait gallery known as the Hall of Governors occupies the second floor corridor that flanks the governor's suite of offices on the south side of the building. The 1982 master plan recommended restoring the second floor corridors and moving the portraits to another location in the Capitol, but these recommendations were not carried out.[72] Instead, when the Executive Chamber was restored in the mid-1980s, the portraits there were moved to the Hall of Governors, and new lighting was installed.[73]

This corridor originally was richly decorated in accord with a scheme developed by H. H. Richardson. The lower part of the walls had reddish-brown Lake Champlain marble wainscoting, and the upper sections were painted a terra cotta color. The mouldings surrounding the doors were enriched with gold, deep red, and dark terra cotta. The corbels and cornice were painted in shades of green, gold, and red.[74] This historic color scheme was reinstated in the fall of 1997. Early in 2007, research was begun to complete the collection of portraits, and the environmental conditions of the corridor were evaluated.[75]

In his first official act, Governor Andrew M. Cuomo issued Executive Order No. 1 on January 1, 2011, reopening the Hall of Governors to the public. Over the course of the next year, the governor worked with historian Harold Holzer, the State Museum, the State Archives, the State Library, the Office of General Services, the Office of Parks, Recreation and Historic Preservation, and organizations including the New York Historical Society and the Albany Institute of History and Art. The objective was to complete the work of locating the missing portraits of governors and to create a museum-quality space for visitors.

In January 2012 Governor Cuomo rededicated the Hall of Governors. Most of the missing portraits had been located. All of the portraits were now hung in chronological order along with biographies of each governor and the artist who had painted the portrait. In addition, cases displaying artifacts relating to many governors' terms of office were placed throughout the hall. In combination with a stenciled timeline along the wall, the new exhibit placed each governor in his historical context. The oldest portrait is of the state's first governor, George Clinton; it was commissioned by the State Legislature in 1813 and painted by Ezra Ames. A portrait of Governor Mario M. Cuomo, painted by Simmie Knox, was added to the collection in June 2013. In February 2014 a portrait of Governor David Paterson was added.

Governor Andrew M. Cuomo unveiled the adjoining new Hall of New York on January 9, 2013. The walls in this area were repaired and painted, and new museum-quality, energy-efficient lighting was installed. This exhibit serves as a counterpoint to the Hall of Governors by focusing on the state's regional diversity, scenic beauty, and its leadership in artistic and cultural affairs. The Hall of New York contains more than 50 paintings on loan from museums, historical societies, and other institutions that illustrate the state's natural and architectural wonders. Visitors can use their smartphones or other digital devices to scan QR codes beside each painting to learn more about the institution that lent the painting.

Hall of Governors

Hall of New York

Original stencil patterns and colors that were revealed
under multiple layers of paint

Demonstration Projects

During the early 1990s the State Commission on the Restoration
of the Capitol initiated several projects to demonstrate other
recommendations from the master plan. Ranging from small
sections of replicated decorative schemes to masonry cleaning,
these projects were intended to raise awareness and to create
an interest in restoring the Capitol. Over the next decade the
first floor and fourth floor corridors, the first floor lobbies, and
many second floor offices, including those of the governor, the
lieutenant governor, and the attorney general, were painted in
historic color schemes.

The Capitol Precinct

The precinct around the Capitol—from Eagle Street on the east
to Swan Street on the west and along Washington Avenue south
to State Street—has been enhanced with improved lighting.
The aluminum cobra-head streetlights were replaced with
forty cast-iron lights that are replicas of ca. 1899 fixtures. The

1879 decorative scheme that was restored in the hallway
in the northeast quadrant of the first floor

New York Power Authority purchased the fixtures on behalf of the OGS using an energy conservation program; the fixtures were then loaned to the city of Albany so that they could be installed, maintained, and energized through the city's existing tariff agreements with the Niagara Mohawk Power Corporation (now part of National Grid). This work was completed early in 2002. In addition, all four facades of the Capitol are now illuminated by high output metal halide lights mounted on 22 foot tall poles; this was also a cooperative project between OGS and the Power Authority and was completed in 2000.[76]

The record of completed restoration projects in the Capitol over the past 35 years is impressive—from the beginnings with the Senate Chamber and continuing through the Great Western Staircase and the elevator and roof projects undertaken by the Office of General Services.

Projects have won awards from the Preservation League of New York State, AIA New York, and Historic Albany Foundation. The roof and skylight projects have been the subject of local PBS documentaries. The *New York Times* and the Albany *Times Union* have published major feature stories.

New streetlights surrounding the Capitol

Capitol facade illuminated

Capitol, west facade and roof

Great Western Stair rendering

NOTES

Chapter One. Chateau on a Hill

1. Frank S. Black, *Public Papers of Frank S. Black, Governor, 1897–1898,* Vol. 2 (Albany: Brandow Printing, 1898), 14–15.

2. Edgar L. Murlin, *The New York Redbook* (Albany: James B. Lyon, 1901), 452.

3. Roswell P. Flower, *Public Papers of Roswell P. Flower, Governor, 1892–[1894],* Vol. 2 (Albany: The Argus Co., 1893–95), 57.

4. *New York Daily Tribune*, December 21, 1896, 6.

5. Most of the work on the Capitol was done by laborers hired on a daily basis. Unlike a contract with a construction firm, there were no deadlines and therefore little incentive to complete work quickly. This day-labor system allowed the legislators to have a hand in the hiring process. Many legislators sought positions for their constituents and were usually listed as providing a recommendation on the roster of workers. This system did allow skilled carvers and stonecutters to be employed for intricate work.

6. Frank S. Black, "Annual Message," in *Messages from the Governors, 1892–1898,* Vol. 9, ed. Charles Z. Lincoln (Albany: J. B. Lyon, 1909), 827.

Chapter Two. Themis Dethroned

1. "New York's Old Capitol," *New York Sun,* Jan. 6, 1879.

2. Ibid.

3. *Laws of the State of New York, Passed at Sessions of the Legislature, 1797, 1798, 1799 and 1800 Inclusive,* Vol. 4 (Albany: Weed, Parsons, 1887), 36.

4. Arthur James Weise, *History of the City of Albany, New York* (Albany: E. H. Bender, 1884), 434.

5. State Laws 1-a, Book 56, *McKinney's Session Laws of New York,* Vol. 1 (St. Paul: West Publishing, 1971), xvii.

6. New York State, Senate, *Documents,* No. 59, 87th Session, 1864, Vol. 4 (Albany: Comstock and Cassidy, 1864), 2.

7. John V. L. Pruyn, April 23, 1863, Personal Journal, [Papers, 1824–1928], Manuscripts Div., NYSL.

8. Cecil R. Roseberry, *Capitol Story,* exp. ed. (Albany: New York State Office of General Services, 1982), 17.

9. John W. Edmonds, *Statutes at Large of the State of New York in the Years 1863, 1864, 1865, 1866,* Vol. 6 (Albany: Weed, Parsons, 1868), 421.

10. New York State, Senate, *Documents,* No. 74, 88th Session, 1865, Vol. 3 (Albany: C. Wendell, 1865), 1.

11. Ibid., 5, 16, 30.

12. Ibid., 9.

13. Ibid., 3–4.

Chapter Three. The Design Competitions

1. For background on the Canadian Parliament buildings, see Carolyn A. Young, *The Glory of Ottawa: Canada's First Parliament Buildings* (Montreal and Buffalo: McGill-Queen's University Press, 1995).

2. Pruyn, May 18, 1866.

3. Pruyn, May 11, 1867.

4. Pruyn, May 13, 1867.

5. New Capitol Commissioners, *Annual Report for 1869* (Albany: The Argus Co., 1870), 27.

6. Pruyn, Aug. 13, 1867.

8. "Annual Report of the New Capitol Commissioners," *Documents of the Senate,* New York State, No. 13, Vol. 1 (Albany: The Argus Co., 1870), 26–27.

8. "Report on the Committee on Finance Relative to Expenditures of the New Capitol," New York State, Senate, *Documents,* No. 95, Vol. 7 (Albany: Weed, Parson, 1875), 1044–45.

9. Pruyn, Nov. 9, 1867.

10. "Memorial of O. B. Latham, February 13, 1868," New York State, Senate, *Documents,* No. 27, Vol. 3 (Albany: C. Van Benthuysen and Sons, 1868), 1–7.

11. Ibid.

12. New Capitol Commissioners, *Annual Report for 1869* (Albany: The Argus Co., 1870), 29–30.

13. Thomas Fuller, "Remonstrance," March 31, 1876, New York State, Assembly, *Documents,* No. 28, Vol. 3 (Albany: Jerome Parmeter, 1877), 62.

Chapter Four. Cornerstone in the Rain

1. Denis Tilden Lynch, *"Boss" Tweed: The Story of a Grim Generation* (New York: Boni and Liveright, 1927), 290.

2. "Another Subject for Investigation—Hon. J. V. L. Pruyn on the New Capitol," *Albany Press,* April 15, 1873.

3. New York State, Assembly, *Documents,* No. 152, Vol. 10 (Albany: Weed, Parson, 1874), 4.

4. "The New Capitol—Laying the First Foundation Stone," *Albany Argus*, July 8, 1869.

5. W. L. McCullough, "Laying of the Cornerstone," manuscript, p. 6, Box 1, Folder 7-2, C. R. Roseberry Collection, Manuscripts Div., NYSL.

6. John T. Hoffman, *Public Papers of the Governor of the State of New York* (Albany: Munsell, 1872), 174.

7. Ibid., 273.

Chapter Five. Battle of the Styles

1. Montgomery Schuyler, "The Work of Leopold Eidlitz—The Capitol at Albany," *Architectural Record*, Nov. 1908, 367.

2. Senate Committee on Finance, "Report Relative to Expenditures of the New Capitol Commissioners," May 20, 1875, New York State, Senate, *Documents,* No. 95, Vol. 7 (Albany: Weed, Parsons, 1875), x.

3. New Capitol Commissioners, "Report Relative to the Plans Submitted by Olmsted, Eidlitz & Richardson," March 3, 1876, New York State, Senate, *Documents* (Albany: Jerome Parmenter, 1876), 4.

4. Ibid., 5.

5. Frederick Law Olmsted to Leopold Eidlitz, July 15, 1875, Olmsted Papers, Library of Congress; photocopy in C. R. Roseberry Papers, Manuscripts Div., NYSL.

6. "The New Capitol at Albany," *New York Daily Tribune,* March 4, 1876, 6.

7. Ibid.

8. Ibid.

9. *American Architect & Building News* 1, March 11, 1876, 81–83.

10. *American Architect & Building News* 2, March 24, 1877, 89.

11. Montgomery Schuyler, "The Capitol of New York," *Scribner's Monthly*, Dec. 1879, 165.

12. Frederick Law Olmsted, April 22, 1876, C. R. Roseberry Papers, Folder 1, Box 9, Manuscripts Div., NYSL.

13. New York Chapter of the American Institute of Architects, "Remonstrance Against the Proposed Changes in the Plans for the Building of the New Capitol," March 29, 1876, New York State, Senate, *Documents* (Albany: Jerome Parmenter, 1876), 1–2.

14. Schuyler, 305.

15. *Albany Argus,* June 15, 1877, 2.

16. Olmsted to Norton, July 20, 1880, C. R. Roseberry Papers, Manuscripts Div., NYSL.

17. C. E. Norton to F. L. Olmsted, April 4, 1876, C. R. Roseberry Papers, Folder 1, Box 9, Manuscripts Div., NYSL.

18. F. L. Olmsted to C. E. Norton, Dec. 27, 1876, C. R. Roseberry Papers, Folder 3, Box 8, Manuscripts Div., NYSL.

19. "The New Capitol," *New York Times,* March 8, 1877, 4.

20. New York State, Senate, *Documents,* No. 44, 100th session, Vol. 2 (Albany: Jerome Parmenter, 1877), 2.

21. Ibid., 3–4.

22. New York State, Senate, *Documents,* No. 47, Vol. 2 (Albany: Jerome B. Parmenter, 1877), 3.

23. *Chronological History of the New Capitol* (Albany: The Press Co., 1879), 10.

24. James F. O'Gorman, *Henry Hobson Richardson and His Office* (Boston: Thomas Todd, 1974), 124.

25. New York State, *Public Papers of Lucius Robinson: Governor of the State of New York* (Albany: The Argus Co., 1877), 57–59.

26. Ibid., 57.

27. Montgomery Schuyler, *American Architecture and Other Writings,* ed. William H. Jordy and Ralph Coe (Cambridge: Harvard University Press, 1961), 177–78.

Chapter Six. Housewarming

1. George Rogers Howell and Jonathan Tenney, *Bi-Centennial History of Albany, 1609–1886* (New York: W. W. Munsell, 1886), 451.

2. Allen C. Beach, *Centennial Celebrations of the State of New York* (Albany: Weed, Parsons, 1879), 416.

3. "The New Capitol," *Syracuse Daily Courier,* Dec. 28, 1878.

4. *Utica Sunday Tribune,* Jan. 12, 1879.

5. "The New Year at Albany," *New York Times,* Dec. 31, 1879.

6. "A Big Festival at Albany," *New York Times,* Jan. 8, 1879, 1.

7. Beach, 424–25.

8. Ibid., 429.

9. Lucius Robinson, "Annual Message*,"* Jan. 7, 1879, *Public Papers of Lucius Robinson, Governor of the State of New York* (Albany: J. B. Lyon, 1879).

Chapter Seven. The Vanishing Murals

1. Helen Knowlton, *The Art-Life of William Morris Hunt* (Boston: Little Brown, 1900), 175.

2. Ibid., 165.

3. Martha Hopper, "Sources and Development of William Morris Hunt's Paintings," in *William Morris Hunt: A Memorial Exhibit* (Boston: Museum of Fine Arts, 1979), 9.

4. Knowlton, 158.

5. Montgomery Schuyler, *American Architecture and Other Writings,* ed. William H. Jordy and Ralph Coe (Cambridge: Harvard University Press, 1961), 178.

6. Knowlton, 175.

7. Knowlton, 177.

8. Quoted in *Utica Morning Herald and Daily Gazette,* Dec. 27, 1878.

9. Henry Adams, "William Morris Hunt's 'Chef d'Oeuvre Inconnu,'" in *Proceedings of the New York State Capitol Symposium* (Albany: Temporary State Commission on the Restoration of the Capitol, 1983), 101.

10. Knowlton, 174.

11. Roseberry, 60.

Chapter Eight. Richardson's Legacy

1. Alonzo B. Cornell, "Annual Message," *Public Papers of Alonzo B. Cornell, Governor of the State of New York* (Albany: E. H. Bender, 1880), 14.

2. New York State, Senate, *Documents,* No. 16, "Annual Report of the New Capitol Commissioners and General Superintendent, For the Year, 1880," Jan. 17, 1881, Vol. 1 (Albany: Weed, Parsons, 1881), 4.

3. James F. O'Gorman, *H. H. Richardson and His Office* (Boston: Thomas Todd, 1974), 123.

4. "The New Senate Chamber," *Harper's Weekly,* April 9, 1881, 236.

5. New York State, Assembly, *Documents,* No. 9, "Report of the Special Committee Appointed by the Assembly of 1879," Vol. 1 (Albany: Weed, Parsons, 1880), 3.

6. New York State, Senate, *Documents,* No. 16, "Annual Report of the New Capitol Commissioners and General Superintendent, For the Year, 1880," Jan. 17, 1881, Vol. 1 (Albany: Weed, Parsons, 1881), 7.

7. "Legislature of New York," *Albany Journal,* March 11, 1881; "The Senate Moving Day," *New York Times,* March 11, 1881, 1.

8. M. E. W. Sherwood, "The Palaces of the People," *Frank Leslie's Popular Monthly,* April 1882, 413.

9. Cornell, 695.

10. "A Throne Room of Justice," *Albany Evening Journal,* Jan. 14, 1884.

11. "Henry H. Richardson," *The New York Star,* April 29, 1886, 2.

Chapter Nine. Isaac Perry Appointed Capitol Commissioner

1. The beginning of this chapter is based on a newspaper story entitled "That Farmer-looking Man," n.d., Isaac G. Perry Scrapbook, 21, C. R. Roseberry Papers, Manuscripts Div., NYSL.

2. Ibid.

3. "Pen Picture of Isaac Perry," n.d., Isaac G. Perry Scrapbook, 2, C. R. Roseberry Papers, Manuscripts Div., NYSL.

4. "A Tour of the Capitol," n.d., Isaac Perry Scrapbook, 49, C. R. Roseberry Papers, Manuscripts Div., NYSL.

5. New York State. *Public Papers of Grover Cleveland, Governor, 1883–1884,* (Albany: The Argus Co., 1883), 24.

6. "The New State Capitol," *New York Times,* May 4, 1884, 5.

7. Isaac Perry, "Report of the New Capitol Commissioner," Jan. 12, 1884, State of New York, Senate, *Documents,* No. 19 (Albany: Wasson and Martin, 1885), 1.

8. While the majority of carving on the Senate Staircase was completed in 1885, the interior diffuser or laylight was not installed until 1896.

9. "The President in Albany," *The New York Sun,* Aug. 11, 1885.

10. New York State, Senate, *Documents,* No. 14, Vol. 2 (Albany: Weed, Parsons, 1884), 8.

11. "To Preserve Our Library," *New York Times,* Feb. 27, 1888, 2.

12. Supervising Commissioners of the Capitol, *Report in Persuance of Chapter 578 of Laws of 1888* (Albany: The Troy Press, 1889), 1.

13. New York State, Senate, *Documents,* No. 13, "Annual Report of the New Capitol Commissioners, 1882," Vol. 1 (Albany: Weed, Parsons, 1883), 5.

14. Isaac Perry, "Communication from the New Capitol Commissioner, May 5, 1884," New York State, Senate, *Documents,* No. 56 (Albany: Weed, Parsons, 1884), 1–2.

15. David B. Hill, *Public Papers of Governor Hill* (Albany: The Argus Co., 1886), 114–20.

16. Capitol Commissioners, *Report for the Years 1891, 1892, 1893 and 1894* (Albany: Wynkoop Hallenbeck Crawford, 1897), 24–25.

17. Commissioner of the New Capitol, *Report for the Year 1885,* 7–9.

18. "The State Capitol," *New York Tribune,* March 6, 1892.

19. Cuyler Reynolds, "The New York Capitol Building," *Architectural Record,* October 1899, 156.

Chapter Ten. Case of the Unfortunate Ceiling

1. New Capitol Commissioners, *Annual Report for the Year 1882* (Albany: Weed, Parsons, 1883), 11–12.

2. Charles Z. Lincoln, ed., *Messages from the Governors of New York State*, Vol. 8 (Albany: J. B. Lyon, 1909), 503.

3. *Rochester Democrat and Chronicle,* Jan. 22, 1888, 4.

4. "The Quarantine Bills," *New York Times,* Jan. 26, 1888, 5.

5. "Its Condition Is Unsafe," *New York Times,* Feb. 4, 1888, 5.

6. "Braced and secure—The Stone Vaulted Ceiling of the Assembly Chamber," *Albany Evening Journal,* [n.d.] 1888, Isaac Perry Scrapbook, Manuscripts Div., NYSL.

7. Leopold Eidlitz to Frederick Law Olmsted, Feb. 4, 1888, photocopy, C. R. Roseberry Papers, Manuscript Div., NYSL.

8. Lincoln, 610.

9. New York State, Assembly, *Documents,* No. 59, Vol. 9 (Albany: Troy Press, 1889), 5.

10. *Brooklyn Daily Eagle,* Jan. 10, 1889, 4.

11. *New York Tribune,* Jan. 18, 1889.

12. New York State, Assembly, *Documents,* No. 59, Vol. 9 (Albany: Troy Press, 1889), 2.

13. Appropriations Committee, *Report Relative to the Matters Connected with the Construction of the Assembly Chamber Ceiling,* Feb. 25, 1889, iii–vii.

14. New York State, Assembly, *Documents,* No. 104, Vol. 14 (Albany: Troy Press, 1889), xii.

Chapter Eleven. The Tower That Never Was

1. New Capitol Commissioners, "Report Relative to the Plans Submitted by Mssrs. F. L. Olmsted, L. Eidlitz, and H. H. Richardson," March 3, 1876, New York State, Senate, *Documents,* No. 49, Vol. 6 (Albany: Weed, Parsons, 1876), 13–21.

2. Charles Elliot Norton to F. L. Olmsted, April 4, 1876, C. R. Roseberry Papers, Folder 1, Box 9, Manuscripts Div., NYSL.

3. "Report of the Capitol Commission, June 4, 1895 to Feb. 15. 1896," New York State, Senate, *Documents,* No. 50, Vol. 7 (Albany: Wynkoop Hallenbeck Crawford, 1896), 9.

4. Ibid., 8.

5. Ibid., 8–9.

6. New York State, Senate, *Documents,* No. 11, Vol. 4 (Albany and New York: Wynkoop, Hallenbeck, Crawford, 1897), 5.

7. Ibid.

8. Report of the Capitol Commission 1895 to 1896, Jan. 29, 1897, New York State, Senate, *Documents,* No. 11, Vol. 4 (Albany: Wynkoop Hallenbeck Crawford, 1897), 5.

Chapter Twelve. The Stone Carvers

1. Capitol Commission, *Annual Report for 1895* (Albany: James B. Lyon), 6–7.

2. "The Governor's Mansion," *New York Daily Graphic,* March 12, 1888, 18.

3. Louis J. Hinton, "Building the State Capitol," Letter to the Editor, *Knickerbocker Press,* Sept. 24, 1921, news clipping, C. R. Roseberry Papers, Manuscripts Div., NYSL.

4. Ibid.

5. Isaac Perry, "Specifications for the Materials and Work Required for Finishing the Construction and Completing the State Capitol at Albany, N.Y.," Feb. 21, 1895, New York State, Senate, *Documents,* No. 43 (Albany: James B. Lyon, 1895), 58.

6. Isaac Perry, "The Great Western Staircase," manuscript, C. R. Roseberry Papers, Folder 7, Box 6, Manuscripts Div., NYSL.

7. Hinton, "Building the State Capitol," Letter to the Editor, *Knickerbocker Press,* Sept. 24, 1921, news clipping, C. R. Roseberry Papers, Manuscripts Div., NYSL.

8. Perry, "The Great Western Staircase," manuscript, C. R. Roseberry Papers, Folder 7, Box 6, Manuscripts Div., NYSL.

9. Ibid.

10. Models were first molded into blue clay and coated with plaster of paris. An additional 1½" of white plaster was applied to the model. The original blue clay was cut away from the back of the model and then the mold was filled with plaster. After drying, the two coatings were cut off and the model was ready for the carver to execute in stone.

11. Edgar L. Murlin, *New York Redbook* (Albany: James B. Lyon, 1895), 464.

12. Ibid., 465.

Chapter Thirteen. Out of the Flames

1. Lela J. Stiles, *The Story of Louis McHenry Howe, The Man behind Roosevelt* (Cleveland: World, 1954), 27.

2. Ibid., 32.

3. "Ruin in the Capitol," *New York Evening Post,* March 29, 1911, NYSL Fire Collection, Box 3, Vol. 2, Manuscripts Div., NYSL.

4. Ibid.

5. Ibid.

6. "Stubborn Fire at State Capitol Destroys Valuable Records," *Albany Argus,* March 29, 1911, NYSL Fire Collection, Box 3, Vol. 1, Manuscripts Division, NYSL.

7. New York State Library, Report of the Director, March 27, 1912, New York State, Assembly, *Documents,* No. 60 (Albany: State University of New York, 1913), 10.

Chapter Fourteen. The Empire State Plaza

1. "Governor Dedicates Mall, Center of Lengthy Dispute" *New York Times,* Nov. 22, 1973, 53.

2. "Corning Calls Takeover by State 'Ruthless,'" *Knickerbocker News,* March 27, 1962, 5A.

3. Ibid.

4. *Press* (Binghamton, NY), March 27, 1962, 2.

5. Samuel E. Bleecker, *The Politics of Architecture: A Perspective on Nelson A. Rockefeller* (New York: The Rutledge Press, 1981), 192.

6. Ibid., 193.

7. "Governor Unveils Cornerstone at $400 Million State Complex," *New York Times,* June 22, 1965, 22.

8. Ibid.

9. "Legislators Pick Art for the Mall," *New York Times,* March 26, 1972, 52.

10. "Errors in Planning of Mall to Cost State $85 Million," *New York Times,* Jan. 27, 1971, 1.

11. "Work on South Mall, the Governor's Rockefeller Center Shakes the Capitol," *New York Times,* Feb. 15, 1968, 45.

12. Martin Filler, "Halicarnassus on the Hudson," *Progressive Architecture* 60 (May 1979): 106–107.

13. "Mall Architecture: Futuristic Doesn't Work," *New York Times,* July 2, 1976, 11.

14. Ibid.

15. Filler, 106.

16. "Mall Architecture," 11.

17. Ibid.

18. "Rocky Gives Wrong Reason for Mall," *Evening News* (Newburgh, NY), Aug. 24, 1970, 8.

19. Ibid.

20. "My Options Open," *New York Times,* Dec. 12, 1973, 97.

21. "After 16 Years, Downtown Albany's Empire State Plaza is Completed," *New York Times,* May 28, 1978, 42.

22. "Mall's Immensity Overwhelms Art Works," *New York Times,* June 24, 1976, 70.

23. "In Marble's White Glare, A Debut for Albany Plaza," *New York Times,* July 2, 1976, 11.

Chapter Fifteen. Restoration of the Capitol, 1977–2013

1. I am very grateful to those who generously shared their recollections and expertise on the restoration and preservation work presented in this chapter: Matthew Bender IV, Douglas G. Bucher, Capitol Architect James Jamieson, Andrea J. Lazarski, John I Mesick, Filip Moens, Justin M. Spivey, and John G. Waite.

2. Chapter 50, *Laws of the State of New York*, 102nd Legislature, 1979, Vol. 1 (Albany: New York State Legislative Bill Drafting Commission, c. 1980), 236–38. Matthew Bender, current chairman of the State Commission on the Restoration of the Capitol, remembers that the Senate had asked the committee on the Senate restoration for advice on how to proceed with the design for a stained glass window in the lobby outside the Senate Chamber after the cartoon for its design had been rejected; a group of commissioners had consulted experts at the Corning Museum of Glass, and that group transitioned into the Commission.

3. *The Master Plan for the New York State Capitol* (Albany: Temporary State Commission on the Capitol, 1982) (hereafter, MP), 84. The historic structure report was prepared by The Ehrenkrantz Group/ Building Conservation Technology.

4. MP, 14.

5. Ibid.

6. MP, 25, 26. For definitions of the terms *restoration, rehabilitation, reconstruction, new construction, new construction, and maintenance,* see p. 25 of the MP.

7. This account of the restoration of the Senate Chamber is based on John I. Mesick, "Restoring the Senate Chamber, 1978–1981," in *Proceedings of the New York State Capitol Symposium* (Albany: Temporary State Commission on the Restoration of the Capitol, 1983), 128–35.

8. The gates were designed and fabricated by metalworker Albert Paley of Rochester. The decorative glass was designed by Hilda Sachs and fabricated by Cummings Studios. Upstairs, in the fourth floor corridor, office partitions had been removed as part of the initial restoration program, and the stonework cleaned. In 2003, the original cut-mosaic tile flooring in the fourth floor lobby was reproduced.

9. This account of the restoration is based on the following documents. MP, 58–59. Mendel, Mesick, Cohen, Waite Architects, Restoration of the Executive Chamber, Project No. M0516, Consultant's Report, Program Phase, Prepared for New York State Office of General Service, Design and Construction Group, 1984. Typescript entitled Executive Summary, Executive Chamber, n.d. "The Executive Chamber of the New York State Capitol," brochure produced by the Temporary State Commission on the Restoration of the Capitol, 1985.

10. As the first step, the consulting architects for the restoration work, Mendel-Mesick-Cohen-Waite Architects, prepared a detailed analysis of the room. During that research many historic images of the chamber were located and then used to guide the restoration.

11. The stained glass was designed by Rowan LeCompte and depicted trees and cultivated crops important to the state; the glass was fabricated by the Greenland Studio and painted by Richard Avidon. The New York Capital District Chapter of the Embroiderers Guild of America stitched ten panels of

intricate gold embroidery for the green mohair draperies. *Threads of the Past, Goldwork in the New York State Capitol,* Vol. 2, ed. Jane Gabriels, Joyce Strand, and Yvonne Welch (Albany: N.Y. Capital District Chapter, The Embroiders Guild of America, 1993), 11–13. The panels were embroidered in 1988.

12. Walter J. Mahoney to Albert Brevetti, May 17, 1982, Memorandum on Rehabilitation of Rooms 123–125.

13. Bud Mahoney to Lauren Vanko, June 15, 1982, Memorandum on Rehabilitation of Rooms 124 and 125.

14. *A Feasibility Study, The New York State Capitol, Rehabilitation and Restoration of the First Floor Public Spaces,* Jan. 1990.

15. The court's discomfort with the Eidlitz courtroom may have been prompted by the structural failures in the Assembly Chamber directly overhead and in the adjoining Golden Corridor. The information on the Court of Appeals is based on the MP, 62–63. Raymond J. Andrews, Scope of Project, Restoration of New York State Capitol, Room 250, for the OGS, Project No. MO518, Dec. 21, 1982-Feb. 2, 1983. Mendel, Mesick, Cohen, Waite Architects, Restoration of the Former Court of Appeals, Project No. M0518, Consultant's Report, Program Phase, Prepared for New York State Office of General Service, Design and Construction Group, 1984. Interview with John I. Mesick, Feb. 21, 2012.

16. The lighting fixtures were altered; the carpeting replaced; and a lighter color scheme introduced.

17. MMCW, Restoration of the Former Court of Appeals, 3.

18. In 1983, Room 250 was reconfigured as a temporary pressroom for the governor's press conferences. The lighting systems needed for television were left exposed in order to minimize damage to the historic fabric of the room.

19. In the 1890s the Grand Army of the Republic used Room 269 to display its Civil War memorabilia. This section is based on the following documents: MP, 38–39, 64–65. "The Governor's Reception Room, The William deLeftwich Dodge Murals, New York State Capitol, Albany," brochure published by OGS, c. 2007. "General Background, Room 269," typescript. "Welcome to Room 269—The Governor's Reception Room," typescript. Andrea J. Lazarski to Henrik Dullea, Dec. 18, 1990.

20. The conservation of the murals was also recommended. Inappropriate infill and lighting were to be removed. Over the next few years there was talk of removing the murals and using the room for press conferences. In 1987 the Legislature appropriated $1.1 million for restoration work, but the project remained stalled.

21. The consultant for the project was Francoise Bollack Architects, working with the staff of the State Commission on the Capitol and the Office of General Services. The Williamstown Art Conservation Laboratory restored the murals in 1995: the surfaces were cleaned and areas of failed paint were stabilized or inpainted. The torchères were fabricated by New Arts Foundry, Baltimore, Md.

22. This section is based on the following: MP, 11, 72–77. Mesick, Cohen, Waite Architects, "Restoration of the Assembly Chamber, New York State Capitol," Aug. 1988–May 1989.

23. Computerized structural modeling carried out in 2003 by Robert Silman Associates indicated that the original sandstone ribbing was drastically overstressed.

24. Some portions of Eidlitz's original ceiling can still be seen in Room 446D.

25. Hunt had painted the murals directly onto the masonry walls rather than on plaster, thereby subjecting them to moisture infiltration.

26. This report was prepared in 1988–89 and led by Mesick Cohen Waite Architects; the report covered the Chamber, its lobbies, and the offices of the speaker and counsel. The report also called

for removing the stone partitions concealing the east and west visitors' galleries, reconfiguring the rostrum, reproducing the door openings and doors, and restoring the original carpeting, light fixtures, and other furnishings. The report further recommended restoring the rooms immediately west of the Chamber to their historic appearance—the Speaker's Office, the speaker's staff and reception room, the west lobby, the legislative counsel's reception and staff office, and the legislative counsel's office. The east lobby was also to be restored.

27. Francois Bollack Architects, working with the staff of the State Commission on the Restoration of the Capitol, were the designers of record. The masonry work was done by Ganem Contracting Corp. and Western Building Restoration. Adam Ross Cut Stone of Albany fabricated the reproduction sandstone balcony for the west gallery. New York State Assembly staff provided project management.

28. The team was led by John G. Waite Associates, Architects, which also restored the East Lobby; Robert Silman Associates were the consulting structural engineer. The vaults would replicate the appearance of the original sandstone and would also help alleviate the original acoustical problems. Within the proposed trusses and supported by them would be space for new offices on the fifth floor. The mechanical and electrical engineering consultants were Plumb Engineering, Excel Engineering, and Plus Group Consulting Engineering. The decorative paint scheme was applied in 2008 by Jan Marie Spanard. The stained glass was conserved by Rohlf's Stained and Leaded Glass Studio in 2007. The torchères were fabricated by Keicher Metal Arts.

29. MP, 72–73, 80. N.Y.S. Commission on the Restoration of the Capitol. Fact sheet on Rooms 342, 341, 343/342A, 306, n.d., 1–3.

30. This work was done under the direction of Francois Bollack Architects, working with the staff of the State Commission on the Restoration of the Capitol. New York State Assembly staff provided project management.

31. This work was done under the direction of Francois Bollack Architects, working with the staff of the State Commission on the Restoration of the Capitol, and by Ganem Contracting Corp. New York State Assembly staff provided project management.

32. The general contractor was the Malatino Construction Corp. Francoise Bollack Architects, working with the staff of the Commission on Restoration of the Capitol, provided architectural services. New York State Assembly staff provided project management.

33. N.Y.S. Commission on the Restoration of the Capitol. Fact sheet on Rooms 342, 341, 343/342A, 306, n.d., 4. The Senate occupied this room while it awaited completion of its chamber.

34. This work was done by Francoise Bollack Architects.

35. MP 72–73, 79. N.Y.S. Commission on the Restoration of the Capitol. Fact sheet on Rooms 342, 341, 343/342A, 306, n.d., 9.

36. Andrea Lazarski, N.Y.S. Commission on the Restoration of the Capitol. Fact sheet on Rooms 342, 341, 343/342A, 306, n.d., 9.

37. Francoise Bollack Architects, working with the staff of the State Commission on the Restoration of the Capitol and OGS, oversaw the project. The general contractor was Ganem Contracting Corp. New York State Assembly staff provided project management.

38. This section is based on the MP, 34, 37; Niklas W. Vigener and James Jamieson, "A Flood of Light: H. H. Richardson's Great Western Staircase at the New York State Capitol," *APT Bulletin: The Journal of Preservation Technology* 39, no. 1 (2008): 9–14; Andrea J. Lazarski, "Great Western Staircase, Preliminary Project Statement, Masonry Cleaning and Lighting," 2002; Mesick Cohen Wilson Baker Architects, Program Phase Report, Improvements to the Great Western Staircase, New York State

Capitol, for N.Y.S. Office of General Services, Design and Construction Group, Project 41288, Dec. 18, 2001; Office of General Services, Great Western Staircase Cleaning Fact Sheet, Jan. 2007.

39. The sampling and analysis was carried out by the Building Research Establishment of Watford, England, and their recommended cleaning methods were tested in 2005. The cleaning and lighting projects were carried out by Mesick Cohen Wilson Baker Architects. The cleaning project was the first to use the Arte Mundit product in North America. Earlier, in 1992, Western Building Restoration and Frances Gale from Masonry Stabilization Services Corporation had carried out a demonstration project to determine the best methods for cleaning the various types of stones used in the staircase. For the lighting project the construction contractor was Monaco Restorations; the electrical engineering consultant was Quantum Engineering Co.; and the electrical contractor was LaCorte Companies. Aurora Lampworks conserved the light fixtures.

40. The consultant team included Simpson Gumpertz & Heger; Ann Beha Architects; Boston Conservation Associates; Cummings Studio; and Titan Roofing.

41. MP, 126. Simpson Gumpertz & Heger, Inc., *Roof Condition Assessment and Master Plan Study, New York State Capitol, Albany, New York,* prepared for the State of New York, Office of General Services, 1998, 1.

42. MP, 126.

43. Simpson Gumpertz & Heger, 3.

44. Ibid., i–ii.

45. Capitol Architect's Report, April 21, 2005.

46. Ibid.

47. Capitol Commission (hereafter, CC), Minutes, July 15, 2008. The work on the west gable was done by Lupini Construction as a separate contract.

48. James Jamieson, e-mail to Diana Waite, Feb. 15, 2012; *Times Union,* June 9, 2012.

49. The design phase engineering work was carried out by engineers Simpson Gumpertz & Heger; Mesick Cohen Wilson Baker Architects were the architectural and historic preservation subconsultants for phase four. Titan Roofing and Monaco Restorations were the contractors for phases one and two, Western Building Restoration for phase three, and Consigli Construction Co. for phase four. Gilban provided construction management for phase four. Superior Clay Tile supplied the terra cotta for phase one, Boston Valley Terra Cotta for phase two, and Gladding McBean for phases three and four. *Times Union,* March 14, 2010; James Jamieson, e-mail to Diana Waite, Aug. 16, 2012.

50. Report of the New Capitol Commission Relative to the Plans Submitted by Messrs. Frederick Law Olmsted, Leopold Eidlitz and H. H. Richardson, N.Y.S. Senate Doc. 49, March 3, 1876.

51. [Lazarski], Restoration of the Assembly Staircase and Skylight, 3–4.

52. Ibid.

53. Ibid., 5–6.

54. Ibid., 9.

55. [Andrea Lazarski], "Senate Staircase," notes. CC, Min., Feb. 9, 2006, 4; CC, Min., July 25, 2006, 4.

56. MP, 36.

57. MP, 34. [Lazarski], Restoration of the Assembly Staircase and Skylight, 6.

58. [Lazarski], Restoration of the Assembly Staircase and Skylight, 4; CC, Min., Dec. 3, 2008, 6. Mickel's stencils, along with his tools and watercolor renderings, are housed at the Albany Institute of

History and Art. EverGreene Studios of New York restored the decorative scheme on the third and fourth story walls. The sandstone was cleaned in 1998 by Western Building Restoration, and the painting of decorative elements on the first through third floors was carried out in 2000 by OGS painters.

59. The consultants were Simpson Gumpertz & Heger; Mesick Cohen Wilson Baker, Architects, also participated in this study.

60. EverGreene Studios decorated the upper sections of the staircase walls. Information on the Assembly Staircase is from PowerPoint presentation by James Jamieson, "The Restoration of the Laylight and Skylight, Assembly Staircase, NYS Capitol," c. 2012.

61. Simpson Gumpertz & Heger, *Program Report, Restoration of Skylights over Assembly and Senate Staircases, New York State Capitol, Albany, NY* (Albany: New York State Office of General Services, 2006), 11–12.

62. CC, Min., Dec. 16, 2006, 2.

63. CC, Min., April 12, 2007.

64. "Some Light Work," *Times Union,* Nov. 4, 2011; Commission on Restoration of the Capitol, Min., Aug. 14, 2007, 4. The construction contract was awarded to Consigli Construction Co. of Milford, Mass., in 2009. Franz Mayor Munich a German firm, fabricated the glass, and the Kuritzky Glass Co. of Mount Kisco, N.Y., handled the installation of both laylights. The Supersky Skylighting System of Wisconsin fabricated and installed both skylights. Gilbane provided construction management.

65. These first elevators were manufactured by the Otis Elevator Company, and the cabs and hoisting apparatus were furnished by the Howard Iron Works of Buffalo. The Senate elevators, located just east of the State Street lobby and the Senate Chamber, were installed by Frederick Tudor and Co. of Boston. The bronze doors and gates were manufactured by the W. S. Tyler Ornamental Iron and Bronze Co. of Cleveland, Ohio, and installed on the first through fourth floors. MP, 132. Plumb Engineering et al, *Upgrade Elevators, New York State Capitol, Project 40801*, prepared for N.Y.S. Office of General Services, Nov. 9, 1998, 9.

66. MP, 132.

67. MP, 132–33.

68. Plumb Engineering et al., 1.

69. The Office of General Services signed a contract in 1997 with Plumb Engineering to study the existing elevators and make recommendations for improvements. Mesick Cohen Wilson Baker Architects and others also participated in the study.

70. This work was done by Bunkoff General Contractors of Latham, N.Y., and completed in 2003.

71. CC, Minutes, Jan. 18, 2008, 2; Dec. 3, 2008, 3. This work was done by Bunkoff General Contracting and Keicher Metal Arts of Leeds, N.Y.

72. MP, 69–70.

73. Commission on the Restoration of the Capitol, Min., July 15, 2008, n.p.

74. Memorandum, Andrea Lazarski to Brad Race, Secretary to the Governor, Nov. 5, 1997.

75. Capitol Architect's Report, April 12, 2007, n.p. Commission on the Restoration of the Capitol, Min., Aug. 14, 2007, n.p.; Jan. 18, 2008, n.p.; Dec. 3, 2008, 8.

76. "OGS Commissioner Ringler Announces Historic Streetlights to Surround State Capitol," OGS Press Release, Jan. 18, 2002.

Assembly skylight rendering

ACKNOWLEDGMENTS

Acknowledgments for the Second Edition

Numerous individuals were helpful in the research for this book, and a few in the loan of rare pictorial material. The author particularly tenders his gratitude to the following: Martin H. Bush, Syracuse, who laid the groundwork by collecting many source documents and photographs; Alfred H. Hallenbeck, former building superintendent, State Capitol; William S. King, former clerk of the Senate for twenty years; Kenneth De Kay, former associate director, Office of Legislative Research; Norman S. Rice, director, Albany Institute of History and Art; Thomas G. Fuller, Ottawa, Ontario, grandson of Thomas Fuller, first architect of the Capitol; Huybertje Lansing Pruyn Hamlin, Albany, daughter of John V. L. Pruyn, member of the original New Capitol Commission; Lucretia Phelps, Binghamton, granddaughter of Isaac G. Perry, last architect of the Capitol; Mrs. Miriam Albee Clausen, Albany, granddaughter of Louis J. Hinton, designer and foreman of carvers on the Western Staircase; Blanche Chadderdon, Catskill, daughter of Otto Baumgartel; Mrs. Gertrude Arenholz, Poughkeepsie, daughter of Killian Drabold, stone-carver on the Western Staircase; Mrs. Carl Koechlin, Athens, N.Y.; Mr. and Cora L. Marx, Albany; Mr. and Genevieve P. Standrod, Albany; William J. Desmond, long-time Capitol guard; Charles S. Kawecki, former state architect; Vincent deP. Martin, assistant to Mr. Kawecki; the staff of the New York State Library for assembling the State Capitol Collection, which will be kept as such in the future;

the Library of Congress; and the Regents of the University of the State of New York. For the use of photographs, particular thanks go to the New York Public Library, New York City; the Albany Institute of History and Art; the Franklin D. Roosevelt Memorial Library at Hyde Park, N.Y.; the Museum of Fine Arts, Boston, Mass.; the Public Archives of Canada, Ottawa, Ontario. The author is also grateful to Charles H. Jennings, director of the Division of Land Utilization, Office of General Services, for special assistance in the 1982 revision of *Capitol Story*.

For valuable assistance in research for the chapter on the Governor Nelson A. Rockefeller Empire State Plaza, special credit and thanks are hereby extended to the following persons: Malcolm Wilson, former Governor of New York; the late Wallace K. Harrison, chief architect of the Empire State Plaza; Dr. William J. Ronan, former secretary to Governor Nelson A. Rockefeller; Isabelle K. Savell, former administrative assistant to Governor Rockefeller; T. Norman Hurd, former director of the budget and director of State operations; Erastus Corning 2nd, Mayor of the city of Albany; General Cortlandt V. R. Schuyler, retired Commissioner, Office of General Services; General Almerin C. O'Hara, former chief of staff to Governor Rockefeller, Adjutant General, and Commissioner of the Office of General Services; Major Edward M. Galvin, N. Y. State Police (retired), former bodyguard to Governor Rockefeller; John C. Byron, former director of construction, Empire State Plaza; Thomas A. Christensen, Manager, Empire State Plaza; James G. Paton, public building manager, Office of General Services; Dr. David Axeirod, Commissioner, State Department of Health; Dr. Hollis Ingraham, former Commissioner, State Department of Health; Albert J. Abrams, former secretary to the Senate; Roger Thompson, former secretary to the Senate; Mark W. Tilley, former executive director, Empire State Performing Arts Center; James Tiberia, executive assistant to the secretary of the Senate; Joan Whitbeck, art administrator, Empire State Plaza; Tammis Groft, Curator, curatorial services, Albany Institute of History and Art; Robert J. Maurer, executive deputy commissioner, State Department of Education; Dr. Robert Fickies, State Geological Survey; Lewis A. Swyer, member, Temporary State Commission on Restoration of the Capitol; Colton D. Harper, former managing director, Eastern Contractors Association; John J. Mesick, architect for the restoration of the Senate Chamber; Walter J. Mahoney, Jr., executive director, Temporary State Commission on the Restoration of the Capitol; David J. Zdunczyk, research assistant on restoration of the Senate Chamber; Paul D. Lightfoot, former assistant coordinator of South Mall construction under General William Wanamaker; Morris Gerber, pictorial historian.

Acknowledgments for the Third Edition

This third edition of *Capitol Story* has been funded by the generous financial support of Furthermore, a program of The J. M. Kaplan Fund; the Gerry Charitable Trust; Richard J. Miller Jr.; Simpson Gumpertz & Heger; the Bender Family Foundation, and Matthew Bender IV. The following institutions have assisted in the publication of this edition: New York State Library, Manuscripts and Special Collections; New York State Archives; New York State Senate Photography; New York State Assembly Photography; Albany Institute of History and Art, and SUNY Press.

Over the last thirty-five years, the restoration of the New York State Capitol was made possible through the cooperation and commitment of the Governor's office and the Legislature. The new edition of *Capitol Story* is a result of the efforts of countless Office of General Services (OGS) employees who contributed to the physical restoration of the building chronicled in the last chapter and helped update and re-edit the book. From architects, historians and administrative staff to custodians, finance managers, and commissioners, OGS has been and will continue to serve as stewards and advocates for this important symbol of New York State democracy.

SELECTED BIBLIOGRAPHY

Beach, Allen C. *Centennial Celebrations of the State of New York*. Albany: Weed, Parsons & Co., 1879.

"A Big Festival at Albany." *New York Times*, Jan. 8, 1879.

Chronological History of the New Capitol. Albany: The Press Co., 1879.

Ehrenkrantz Group. "New York State Capitol Historic Structure Report," 1983. New York State Library, Manuscripts and Special Collections, Albany, New York.

Hitchcock, Henry-Russell. *The Architecture of H. H. Richardson and His Times*. Cambridge and London: MIT Press, 1966.

Holiday, Kathryn E. *Leopold Eidlitz: Architecture and Idealism in the Gilded Age*. New York: W. W. Norton & Co., 2008.

Hopper, Martha. "Sources and Development of William Morris Hunt's Paintings." In *William Morris Hunt: A Memorial Exhibit*. Boston: Museum of Fine Arts, 1979.

Howell, George Rogers, and Jonathan Tenney. *Bi-Centennial History of Albany, 1609–1886*.

New York: W. W. Munsell & Co., 1886.

Knowlton, Helen. *The Art-Life of William Morris Hunt*. Boston: Little Brown & Co., 1900.

Landsam, Walter E. "The New York State Capitol: Evolution of the Design, 1866–1876." Master's thesis, Yale University, 1968.

Mendel Mesick Cohen Architects. "The New York State Senate Chamber and Related Spaces, A Historic Structure Report," 1978.

Mercer, Paul, and Vicki Weiss. *The New York State Capitol and the Great Fire of 1911*. Charleston, S.C.: Arcadia Publishing, 2011.

Murlin, Edgar L. *New York Redbook*. Albany: James B. Lyon, 1901, 452–472.

"The New Capitol at Albany." *New York Daily Tribune*, March 4, 1876.

"The New Senate Chamber." *Harper's Weekly*, April 9, 1881.

New York State Library Fire Collection, 1899–1942. New York State Library, Manuscripts and Special Collections.

New York State New Capitol Commission. Plans and drawings pertaining to the construction of the State Capitol, ca. 1869–1900. New York State Library, Manuscripts and Special Collections.

"The New Year at Albany." *New York Times*, Dec. 31, 1879.

O'Gorman, James F. *Henry Hobson Richardson and His Office*. Boston: Thomas Todd Co., 1974.

Ochsner, Jeffrey Karl. *H. H. Richardson: Complete Architectural Works*. Cambridge: MIT Press, 1984.

Proceedings of the New York State Capitol Symposium. March 14–16, 1981. Albany: Temporary State Commission on the Restoration of the Capitol, 1983.

Pruyn, John Van Schaick Lansing, Papers, 1824–1928. New York State Library, Manuscripts and Special Collections.

Reynolds, Cuyler. "The New York Capitol Building." *Architectural Record* 19 (Oct. 1899): 142–187.

Roseberry, Cecil R., Papers. New York State Library, Manuscripts and Special Collections.

Schuyler, Montgomery. "The Capitol of New York." *Scribner's Monthly* 19 (Dec. 1879): 165.

Schuyler, Montgomery. "The Work of Leopold Eidlitz, The Capitol at Albany." *Architectural Record* 24 (Nov. 1908): 365–378.

Sherwood, M. E. W. "The Palaces of the People." *Frank Leslie's Popular Monthly* 13 (April 1882): 408–413.

Temporary State Commission on the Restoration of the Capitol. *The Master Plan for the New York State Capitol*. Albany: Temporary Commission on the Restoration of the Capitol, 1982.

Webster, Sally. *William Morris Hunt*. New York: Cambridge University Press, 1991.

Weise, Arthur James. *History of the City of Albany, New York*. Albany: E. H. Bender, 1884.

Young, Carolyn A. *The Glory of Ottawa: Canada's First Parliament Buildings*. Montreal and Buffalo: McGill-Queen's University Press, 1995.

INDEX

Note: *Italicized* page numbers indicate material in captions.